BONE OF MY BONES
and
FLESH OF MY FLESH

JOSÉ U. RIVERA

Bone of My Bones and Flesh of My Flesh

GOD'S MASTER PLAN FOR FAMILY, HOME AND CHURCH

Oikos Ministries Global | Pastor José Uriel Rivera Collazo

Pastor José U. Rivera
Riveraju2900@gmail.com

All rights reserved.

No part of this book may be reproduced without the written authorization of the author, except as provided by the United States of America Copyright Law

©Oikos Ministries Global/José U. Rivera 2017

Unless otherwise indicated, all scripture quotations are from the King James Version of the Holy Bible.

Conventions used: Brackets, Italics, Bold or other emphasis are solely the authors.

Contents

Dedication	| 07
Acknowledgements	| 09
Foreword	| 11
Personal Letter to the Reader	| 15
Introduction	| 21
CHAPTER 1. Triunity	| 23
CHAPTER 2. The Sixth Day Dirt and Dust: God Gets Personal	| 27
- Dirt	| 28
- Dust	| 32
- Man	| 33
CHAPTER 3. Spiritual DNA	| 38

CHAPTER 4. Understanding Relationships	41
CHAPTER 5. God The Gardener	43
CHAPTER 6. What's In a Name?	47
CHAPTER 7. Being Alone Is Not Good	53
CHAPTER 8. A Promise of Help	55
CHAPTER 9. A Surgical Procedure by Dr. God	59
CHAPTER 10. A Woman in the Making	63
CHAPTER 11. Bone of My Bone and Flesh of My Flesh	73
CHAPTER 12. She Shall be Called Eve	83
CHAPTER 13. Honoring the Woman – A Forgotten Perspective	85
CHAPTER 14. Disobedience – The Inception of Sin	89
CHAPTER 15. The Persona of Satan – Agent of Sin	95

CHAPTER 16.
The Agent of Sin Strategizes Against God and the Future of Humanity | 105

CHAPTER 17.
Not Just Any Tree – Not Just Any Fruit | 113

CHAPTER 18.
Desire/Lust – Key to Unlocking Knowledge of Good and Evil | 117

CHAPTER 19.
Humanity's and Satan's Trial Begins | 125

CHAPTER 20.
Jesus the Second Adam | 133

CHAPTER 21.
The Gift | 139

CHAPTER 22.
The Family and the Bible | 145

CHAPTER 23.
The bride of Jesus the Divine | 149

CHAPTER 24.
Responsibilities of the Wife and the Husband | 155
-     Companionship | 156

CHAPTER 25.
True Love - 1 John 4 | 169

CHAPTER 26.
Sexual Intimacy and Children | 171

CHAPTER 27.
Keeping It Together | 175

CHAPTER 28.
Church Leadership and the
Marriage Relationship | 181

CHAPTER 29.
An Appeal from Christ to All Men | 195
- Your Mom | 195
- Your Responsibility to your Wife | 197

CHAPTER 30.
An Appeal from Christ to All Women | 183

CHAPTER 31.
God's Family | 209

Dedication

First, I dedicate this work to Elohim without whose Master Plan, I would not have been born to write about it.

Second, I dedicate it in honor of my beloved mom, Margarita Collazo Oquendo and to my dad, José Rivera Marrero. Mom was responsible for introducing me, as a child, to Christ Jesus, my Savior and Lord.

Third, I dedicate it to my wife Claudia, whose untiring encouragement and faith that this was God's plan, pressed on, until its completion. Since it was first conceived, she and my Mother-in-Law, Daysi, prayed and moved many people, to pray and bless the project and those who would benefit from it.

Fourth and equally as important, my children: Michelle, Yasmin and Alex and my present and future grandchildren: Daniel, Jonathan, Nathaniel, Matthew, Gavri'el and Mikah'el theirs will be the generation that makes the difference.

BONE OF MY BONES and FLESH OF MY FLESH / 08

Acknowledgements

Blessed are those who in some form, big or small, have made an impact upon my life and have encouraged me to put down in words, the thoughts, contemplations, reflections of this manuscript.

As the ink dries upon this page, and your name is mirrored in contrast to the color of the paper, you honor God and me for this work to be a legacy for generations.

My blood brothers and sisters: Delia, Sonia, Federico, Orlando, Rebecca, Arnaldo, Laura, Hector, Alice, Waida and my "Little B", Belinda, who is resting and waiting upon the Lord, for the trumpet to sound and celebrate the Wedding Feast of the Lamb.

Fivefold Ministry Partners, and their wives whose encouragement and friendship continue to be a source of inspiration in the life of my wife and I: Pastor Edward Gutierres, his wife Norma and their Children; our first Oikos house church; Pastor Femi Adun and Busola, Grace House, London England; Cesar Morales and Sandra,

Hechos TV, Orlando, FL; Pastor Eric Melwani and Janet, Church of Many Waters, Orlando, FL; Pastor Francisco Rodriguez (Paquito) and Raquel, Multicultural Theological Institute/Orlando Southeast, AG; Pastor Joe Maese and Soledad, Phoenix, AZ.

My Spanish and English students at the Multicultural Theological Institute/Orlando Southeast, AG; Classes: Pentateuch, Daniel, Revelation, Pastoral Epistles, Holy Spirit.

My Arizona in-law-family Mami Daysi, Natalia, Mario and Carlos who always go out of their way to make sure my wife and I are very well taken care of.

May God's grace and favor be with you all, for the rest of your lives. Thank you.

Foreword

In nearly two decades of walking with and for the Lord Jesus Christ, I have held tightly to the school of thought, that it will be difficult and impossible for the church or any nation, to fulfil God's grand plan without an in-depth study and understanding of God's plan and purpose, for the family institution. In the first three chapters of the Bible, we read the unfolding of God's agenda for the entire earth to be restored and replicated to look exactly like the culture of heaven; hence, the phrase heaven on earth. Unfortunately, the failure of the first family abiding by God's precepts, led the entire human race in an entirely different direction from what God intended. Adam and Eve's disobedience made them vulnerable. This gave Satan, the enemy of anything good, the opportunity to introduce his destructive agenda.

Tranquillity, Equality, Unity and the Prosperity of all men and women, young or old, was and is still part of God's plan for the entire human race. However, I believe it is inappropriate to attempt the pursuance of this course, without looking and catering for the family's institution, as you may agree with me, which is the foundation or the bedrock of civilised or uncivilised society. My conviction for this parallel, is based simply on the written word of God, authenticated by several historical facts, and my personal experience of being part of the nuclear family, as well as a spiritual (The Church) family.

As a pastor, I was once preparing to give a speech during a Father's Day Convention. I found a report, posted by The Centre for Social Justice in the United Kingdom. The report detailed the staggering statistics of fatherlessness; a fast rising issue within the British Isles. This, resulted in the psychological imbalance of many teenagers, causing the increase of several social upheavals, thereby threatening the goal of safe communities in most Boroughs across the United Kingdom.

The report further stated, that family policy is best summed up in one statistic – 48 percent of all children born today, will see the breakdown of their parents' relationship (Forgotten Families? The vanishing agenda, 4th October 2012). This piece of information, is heart breaking and should stir up conversations within the Christendom, leading to initiatives such as this book you have in your hands right now. It will provide information and solutions from biblical perspectives, to cob this nemesis ravaging our society, in turn, destabilising the foundations of our nations.

In this book, Pastor José Rivera has not only written intelligently but has spiritually answered the question many individuals in today's 21st-century world are asking regarding marriage and faith. He cautiously and exegetically argued his view-point, of the impact of marriage on every aspect of society and human endeavour, especially the faith life in God. This masterpiece is not a book; it's a life manual for building a godly and productive marriage relationship. While it draws focus from marriage; it also provides beneficial and vital information for establishing a robust and healthy family.

In over half a decade that I have known and had the privilege of spending several days and nights, conversing with Pastor José on several issues that bother on every aspect of life, he has continued to deliver exceptional wisdom and cutting-edge knowledge of all these subject matters; many that have significantly imparted knowledge into my soul, as well as direction for decision making. It therefore, gives me so much confidence, that each page in this life manual, will not only set the mind of each reader on fire but will also relieve the soul of stress from marital pressures or family difficulties.

I congratulate you sir! This book has blessed me. I have no doubt it will have the same effect on millions of people that will read it across the nations of the earth, in several languages. I pray this will be the first book amongst much MORE.

Apostle Femi Adun
President/Founder
Eagle World Outreach, UK

BONE OF MY BONES and FLESH OF MY FLESH / 14

Personal Letter to the Reader

Dear Beloved Reader:

Thank you for acquiring this book.

Your choice, indicates your search for knowledge and wisdom beyond what has already been poured into your mind.

Perhaps you are just curious and have questions that may be answered by some content in the book. Whatever your reason, I believe the Holy Spirit, has led you here.

Whether you agree with me or not, the purpose of God for your life, ministry or spiritual endeavor, requires your gleaning the information within these pages, for a change in your life or the impartation of change in the life of others.

God's Master Plan takes into account all contingencies. Even before you and I were in existence, the purpose and causeway of our lives was taken into consideration. Provision of resources was allocated, so that we would fit-in with God's perfect plan, in order to leave a legacy of faith, belief, truth and witness to His existence and love for humanity.

Without a personal knowledge of God, you will only receive from this book some intellectual gratification that will fill your need for the present.

If you have an existing relationship with God, the material supplied will only enhance that relationship but may not satisfy your soul. You seek knowledge and understanding but your love of God has not yet matured.

If you are seeking to please God in your relationship with him, then your love for him and his love for you will harmonize. The gratification will come in an inexorable euphoria of spiritual manifestation that will delight, nourish and fulfill a wanting soul. A soul content with a daily dosage of the indwelling glory of Christ in you.

None of us are perfect in our own understanding. [*Romans 3:10 "…as it is written, There is none righteous, no, not one."*]

We all sin every day. [*Romans 3:23 "…for all have sinned, and fall short of the glory of God…"*]

We carry guilt for things that speak ill of us. We carry a closet of skeletons worthy of any good graveyard. [*Romans 3:12 'They have all turned aside, they are together become unprofitable; There is none that doeth good, no, not, so much as one.'*]

We don't want to expose ourselves in any way because of what others will think or say about us. We don't want to hurt the ones we love. We prefer to shelter them or us, from the proportional size of our sins.

We pay handsomely to psychiatrists, psychoanalysts, counselors, psychologists and often beyond our means, to seek truth, direction, or an empathic being who will listen to the confessions of the perverse machinations and desires of our sinful hearts. Yet, there seems to be no adequate solution. So, we keep delving deeper and deeper into our own pool of desperation. Only the grave, becomes the shrine for the once human being, with hopes and aspirations, which were never carried out. Empty hands, which will be displayed before the Creator, with no apparent reason for an unaccomplished lifetime.

While we live, there is still hope. Jesus said it best: [*Matthew 11:28 Come unto me, all ye that labor and are heavy laden, and I will give you rest.*] [*"Revelation 3:20 Behold, I stand at the door and knock: if any man hear my voice and open the door, I will come in to him, and will sup with him, and he with me."*]

You've probably heard about Jesus the Christ, sometime in your life and upon reading this you say "this is another religious sales pitch."

My intent, is not to have you do anything you don't want to. I would only love for you to have a relationship with Christ, as I have for a lifetime. He has been my friend and mentor. He introduced me to the Holy Spirit, who now dwells in me. He gave me an understanding of the Word, that allows me share it with you, as a friend. Your decisions are strictly yours. I would love it, if one day, instead of occupying a graveyard plot, you would join Christ and I, at his wedding feast with the Saints.

If you consider a change, from your present state of mind, allow me to offer a simple prayer you can say in the privacy of your quiet place.

"Lord Jesus, I am fully aware that I have sinned and ask your forgiveness at this very moment. I understand that I may sin again at some point in my relationship with you. [*1John 2:1, 2 "My little children, these things write I unto you that ye may not sin. And if any man sin, we have an Advocate with the Father, Jesus Christ the righteous: and he is the propitiation for our sins; and not for ours only, but also for the whole world."*]

Please give me strength to be a better person and guide me through your Word, so that I may never sin again.

Please help me make my house a home, with you as our unseen guest.

Restore my relationship with my wife/ husband/ children/ stepchildren, etc. that I may be an example of your everlasting love.

Thank you for your grace and mercy. Amen!"

Keep in mind, that Christianity is not a religion. It is a lifestyle of service after Christ. Men will fail; even ones who have or are serving God. None of us is exempt from sin. The enemy makes sure that we set bad examples for others.

Look to Christ. He is the perfect example. He has never failed. He will satisfy you like no one else can. He was looking ahead and believed in you, to the point of taking the wrath of God upon himself, so that you will have the opportunity of everlasting life. [*1Peter 2:24 "He took our sins on himself, giving his body to be nailed on the tree, so that we, being dead to sin, might have a new life in righteousness, and by his wounds we have been made well".*]

May God continue to bless you, your home and family, every day of your life.

I would love to hear from you.

Please send your questions or confirmation of the above prayer to God. Write to me at riveraju2900@gmail.com . I want to continue praying and celebrating every milestone in your Christian journey.

Your friend and co-laborer in Christ,
Pastor Jose Uriel Rivera Collazo.

BONE OF MY BONES and FLESH OF MY FLESH / 20

Introduction

[2Timothy 3:16 "Every Scripture is inspired by God and is useful for teaching, for convincing, for correction of error, and for instruction in right doing; so that the man of God may himself be complete and may be perfectly equipped for every good work."]

The contents of this book, is something which the Spirit of God has been motivating me to write about, for a time. I have written many things before for small groups but never at the stage of publishing for a wider audience.

I have debated in my mind, as to how many times, a subject of this nature, has been written about and why my inspiration would perhaps make a difference. I decided just to be obedient and follow the leading of the Holy Spirit. This is His work and those in need, will be led to it.

Bone of my Bone and Flesh of my Flesh, came to me, as a revelation from studying Scripture. It came as a result of answering many questions for couples in ministry and secular life, about husband/wife, family relationships and how to be an effective leader, in the home and in the church. The questions and the answers, always took me back to the beginning.

I have served God all my life. He is my mentor, friend, comforter in times of trouble; he is my first consult in prayer and His Word, and my final reference for answers. I keep the Bible as my answer book because in it, I have discovered God always has an answer based on His plan, from the beginning.

Sin nature interrupted the way men think and act regarding the challenges of life. Man thinks he knows it all and continues to try and prove it. He uses science in all its capacity, to unlock many mysteries. Man forgets, that science is a gift of God. All the elements of man's discovery on the planet, are clues placed there by the Creator. Their discovery, was intended for the emergence of natural man, into his supernatural eternal destiny, demonstrated by God's son, Christ Jesus.

Because we seem to have forgotten our proper place in the original plan, is perhaps the reason for this book. It may not be a scholarly or academic endeavor, drenched with exquisite choice narrative but it will be suitably accommodated by the Holy Spirit, to the needs of the inquisitive soul. Are you teachable? Read on. Let me know what you think. Read with an open mind and a willing spirit. Your new lifestyle is about to unfurl.

TRIUNITY

God's circle of life, has no beginning and no end. The glory of eternity, was shared only by the Triunity: Father, Son, and Holy Spirit.

I use the term Triunity because it is the willful cooperation of God's nature, to present an identity to mankind, which would relate with his own, for all of civilization. It has never been about questioning His attributes, personality, gender and purpose. It has always been about us, in relationship to him. [*Isaiah 29:16 "Ye turn things upside down! Shall the potter be esteemed as clay; that the thing made should say of him that made it, He made me not; or the thing formed say of him that formed it, He hath no understanding?"*]

You may ask yourself "how is it that you come to this conclusion, since theologians have always presented Trinity over Triunity"?

The answer is revealed in the Bible. In God's own declaration, before the nation of Israel, in the "shemA". You and I have come to know this, in the western world as

BONE OF MY BONES and FLESH OF MY FLESH / 24

[*Deuteronomy 6:4 "Hear, O Israel: The LORD our God is one LORD."*]

In the Hebrew language it is written: *"shemA Yisrael, Yehovah Eloheinu, Yehovah achaD"*. In this statement, Yehovah refers to himself as *"Eloheinu"*, the Creator; or as we know him, God and Lord. In the same sentence he refers to himself as *"achaD"* or as one. God therefore is plural in nature and works as one entity. By His prime example, we are plural: spirit, soul and body and work as a Triunity of willful cooperation, in carrying out the Master Plan.

In His Master Plan, before our existence, they were the force of creation, to the things we see and to the things we have yet to see. They had created powerful eternal servants with differing ranks, levels of authority and with limited lifetimes, in relationship to the Triunity. The purpose of these eternal servants known as Cherubim, Seraphim, Archangels and Angels, was to assist with service to the Triunity and this new creation. This was the Master Plan.

> In His Master Plan, before our existence, The Triunity were the force of creation, to the things we see and to the things we have yet to see.

The Master Plan incorporated new life and civilizations, worlds, galaxies and a pathway to Triunity. There would be heavens, diverse planes of existence, light, darkness, elements to be discovered and the Triune collective conscience, feeding the knowledge and wisdom, for this infinite process of creation to be born, according to the Master Plan.

The Triunity, having no reference of time in eternity, needed a new set of governing rules, to be implemented. These new rules involved the sustainment of life outside of the Triunity. All the harmony which made them the collective Triunity, would have to be transmitted, to this new creation. It had to be birthed in love. It had to be personal. It needed to be a reflection of the collaboration of the Triunity. It required an overseer. That overseer, need to be able to love, care and be responsible, for all life. This Lord of the new creation, needed to transcend into that Triune collective existence. It needed a will. It required to be conscious of itself and the rest of creation. It needed the ability of independent thought, with relationship to its created habitat. It needed to understand life, love, relationship, authority, dominion and its Creator.

There would have to be a starting point. A centrally located axis for this Genesis. To this task, they set their mind as one God. They take into account all present and future contingencies. The Holy Spirit makes the introduction.

> [*Genesis 1:1, 2 "In the beginning God created the heaven and the earth. And the earth was without form, and void; and darkness was upon the face of the deep. And the Spirit of God moved upon the face of the waters".*]

So, the "beginning", did not have a time reference point, because the time markers, had not been set in their causeway, in the Master Plan. In other words, the sun, moon and stars had not started their prescribed orbit. It is at this juncture, that the words of the writer in Genesis describes the general events leading to creation, within the Master Plan:

> [*Genesis 1:3, 4 "And God said, Let there be light: and there was light. And God saw the light, that it was good: and God divided the light from the darkness".*]

From Genesis 1:5-23, we see God calling things into existence. The first 5 days of creation are accounted for. On the sixth day, something interesting happens. Let's review the account.

THE SIXTH DAY – DIRT AND DUST: GOD GETS PERSONAL

[Genesis 1:25-31 "<u>And God made</u> the beast of the earth after his kind, and cattle after their kind, and everything that creeps upon the earth after his kind: and God saw that it was good.

And God said, <u>Let us make man in our image</u>, after our likeness: and let them have dominion over the fish of the sea, and over the fowl of the air, and over the cattle, and over all the earth, and over every creeping thing that creeps upon the earth. So <u>God created man in his own image, in the image of God created he him; male and female created he them</u>. And God blessed them, and God said unto them, be fruitful, and multiply, and replenish the earth, and subdue it: and have dominion over the fish of the sea, and over the fowl of the air, and over every living thing that moves upon the earth. And God said, Behold, I have given you every herb bearing seed, which is upon the face of all the earth, and every tree, in the which is the fruit of a tree yielding seed; to you it shall be for meat. And to every beast of the earth, and to every fowl of the air, and to everything that creeps upon the earth, wherein there is life, I have given every green herb for meat: and it was so.*

And God saw everything that he had made, and, behold, it was very good. And the evening and the morning were the sixth day".] (KJV)

Dirt

It is in the 6th day, that God becomes personally involved with his creation. We read "*And God made the beast of the earth after his kind*". God made the animals of the planet and man, from the dirt. More specifically of the man, he is made of the dust of the earth. (More on the dust just ahead.)

Everything that God does, has a pattern and follows His specific plan. To be made, involves a personal process of hands on. Things are made for a reason and for a purpose. In this case, anything that was going to have God's spirit of life, had to be personal. It was a part of God's being, which would demonstrate his character and nature.

Anyone who has made something with their hands, looks to it with pride. A child's first painting or drawing, a dress, a cake, a book case; anyone involved with these and other projects, does not set out to make mistakes. There is purpose, reason, form, function, design, and intellectual formulation. You want it done well, because it reflects your accomplishment, it is who you are. God made it personal.

> Everything that God does, has a pattern and follows His specific plan. To be made, involves a personal process of hands on. Things are made for a reason and for a purpose.

29 / The Sixth Day – Dirt and Dust: God Gets Personal

God's direct involvement in "making", demonstrates several things. It demonstrates that God works. He is not idly sitting by or letting anyone else, do what he is responsible for. He teaches us, the importance of work and "making". He shows us, how to take ownership of our own making. As He takes responsibility for every aspect of creation, we should do the same, by following His example.

Animal or human life are both important to God. They are personal to Him. God gave the Lord of this new creation, dominion over it. God disapproves, in the unwanted taking of any life. In the elimination of any life, you are hurting, despising and throwing away a part of His spirit. He is the life within all created beings. To take your own life or someone else's, is thoughtless and disrespectful of the life we all share.

> [1Corinthians 6:19 "*Or do you not know that your body is the temple of the Holy Spirit who is in you, whom you have from God, and you are not your own?*"]

Once God had completed making the animals, he proceeds to make man. Here, we need to refer to the Scripture and observe closely, how the sentence is grammatically constructed. The importance lays, in all the different arguments presented by scholars, academicians, theologians and the like. I just want you to see it, from what I feel, was God's perspective.

> [*Genesis 1:26, 27* "<u>And God said,</u> <u>Let us make man in our image,</u> <u>after our likeness</u>: *and let them have dominion over the*

fish of the sea, and over the fowl of the air, and over the cattle, and over all the earth, and over every creeping thing that creeps upon the earth. <u>So God created man in his own image, in the image of God created he him</u>; male and female created he them."]

"And God said…"

Every time I see this phrase, I ask myself one question. If God is this powerful, why does he have to 'say' anything? Couldn't he have just willed it into existence?

At that very moment, the Holy Spirit, to whom I have given dominion over my human thinking, answers and says. He is God and he can do anything he sovereignly wants to. He is calling these out, for the human benefit. Because this is the beginning of all things created, he wants to show humanity that faith, is the substance of things called for and the demonstration of things not seen. This is the law for the natural realm.

By calling things as they are, God shows us the purpose of confession, in faith. As humans, we can think about something and it will not materialize because we thought about it. Humans have to make a determination. They need to confess what it is that they want. Whether through prayer, supplication, plea or declaration, what you declare out loud causes the Creator to work with your faith to make things happen. As you call out the unseen in faith, you show God that you are following his example. God will then release the substance/the resources, to grant your request.

31 / The Sixth Day – Dirt and Dust: God Gets Personal

Our next phrase is *"Let us make..."*

Here, God initiates the spirit of cooperation. The Triunity is involved: the **"us"**. It cannot be the created eternal servants; namely Cherubim, Seraphim, Archangels or Angels because they are in fact, created beings. The Master Plan calls for the Triunity, to develop the Master Plan.

The subsequent phrase is *"man in our image..."*

The word image, conjures up all sorts controversies, because our minds are trained to think on a carnal and/or a spiritualized form. Notice I did not say spiritual! If God is speaking as the collective Triunity, what image is He talking about? We certainly don't look or act, the part of gods. There are a few selfish humans, who would like nothing more than to have the power of a god, to form a dictatorship or some self-grandiose scheme, to subject humanity to worship at their feet. (By the way, this was tried in heaven already and it failed.)

The term *"image"* to me, in this case, would refer to God's own imagination and design. No one has ever seen God. Why would God put his image on a lesser being?

Keep in mind that the Triunity has a Master Plan. Where it concerns humanity, the omniscience of God foresaw every contingency. In order to make the man, the Triunity not only thought of the present, they took into consideration the future. God's creation was good. God knew the eventual downfall of man. His contingency plan included redemption and restoration. As a result, the image placed on the man was that of a living soul. Not just any soul but the image (the traits and characteristics) of His son. The form of humanity, would be a walking, talking temple. It would eventually be, the temporary habitation of the Triunity. It would be the way of personal identification with pain, sorrow, love and every other carnal manifestation that would need to be redeemed and restored. The image had to be made from the earth, in order to redeem the planet, humanity and the animals. It needed to have a divine soul for the eventual redemption of all souls through Christ. The image had to be perfect and God saw it was good.

The next phrase is *"our likeness…"*

To me this simply means everything that the Triunity likes and that which they dislike. If this man, was to be the representative of the Triunity in this new creation, according to the Master Plan, he needed to personify his Creator. In this four dimensional universe, man would conform to God's likeness. Not as God; like a god.

"Let them have dominion…" As in the Triunity's eternal universe, everything conforms to their dominion, so in this created universe, man and woman were given dominion over it.

Therefore *"God created man in his own image, in the image of God created he him; male and female created he them"*.

Dust

> *[Genesis 2:7 "And the LORD <u>God formed man of the dust of the ground,</u> and <u>breathed into his nostrils the breath of life;</u>*

and <u>man became a living soul</u>".]

As we read before, we see God as the Triunity, creating the animals, everything that creeps on, and in the ground, flies over, or lives under water. It even says he created man and woman and gave them dominion.

Why then, in Genesis Chapter 2, does God make mention that he made man from the dust of the earth? It is a perplexing question and one that needs answering. As a matter of fact, we will be looking at three perspectives, of the verse quoted above.

In Jewish literature, we find that often things are repeated backwards and forwards and even two or three times. I have come to understand, in speaking with one Jewish teacher, that repetition aids memory and that is why, in the book of Psalms, similar to the way we write music today, the lines are repeated in order to remember the song or its meaning made clearer.

It is my belief that the first two chapters of Genesis present us with an outline of creation. In Chapter one, an abbreviated outline and a more detailed outline in Chapter 2. We see a similar pattern in the book of Revelation, Chapters 1 and 2.

Man

Ok. The first phrase - *And the LORD <u>God formed man of the dust of the ground</u>*. So, why the dust?

We have dust all over, in our daily living. We all pay dearly for the cleaning of it. We have even given it endearing names, such as "dust bunnies". What is so intriguing about dust, that God would even use it to create man? God would need a reason to allow the writer to use this term. It would have some significance to the reader. What is God teaching from the beginning?

Dust does nothing but accumulate. Dust just lays in place. Dust becomes active, when some form of air pressure acts upon it.

We have a tendency to blow it off with our breath, or in today's society, with canned air or a reverse vacuum, as a blower. We don't like it when we are cleaning and a gust of wind, or someone, comes by and ruins the beautiful job of cleaning we performed.

Are you getting the picture yet? Dust is alive only when it receives a breath of air. In other words, man was to understand, that as he was made from the dust of the earth, his life would be limited to God's active life force, his Spirit, which would keep him alive. If you were to strike a dusty place, it would in a sense make the dust alive and it would go everywhere. In a few moments, the dust would settle back again somewhere, until it was activated again. So, the created Lord of this new world, was to understand that his body was dust. It would rise like the dust and would settle like the dust, back to its dormant state.

> [Genesis 3:19 "In the sweat of thy face shalt thou eat bread, till thou return unto the ground; for out of it were thou taken: for dust thou art, and unto dust shalt thou return".]

God even used dust to create lice.

> [*Exodus 8:17* "...*for Aaron stretched out his hand with his rod, and smote the dust of the earth, and it became lice in man, and in beast; all the dust of the land became lice throughout all the land of Egypt*".]

Dust, would be to man, a perpetual reminder that his physical body was made and activated, as the dust of the earth. From it he was made and to it he would return.

> [*Job 34:15* "*All flesh shall perish together, and man shall turn again unto dust*".]

> [*Ecclesiastes 12:7* "*Then shall the dust return to the earth as it was: and the spirit shall return unto God who gave it*".]

Continuing with the above verse (Genesis 2:7), we come to the second of the three phrases, with God's personal involvement, in the making of man: <u>breathed into his nostrils the breath of life…</u>

Why would this Triune God, breathe upon this earthen form and specifically through the nostrils? As God, he could have just waved his hand or some other gesture to bring man into life.

I believe, the answer to the question, goes back to God's love for all created life and personal relationship, with the man he was creating. To breathe upon the man, meant that this breathing process, was special. All other created forms were already breathing and alive by God's own command. This act, was a demonstration of God's favor and grace. It was a personal impartation of God's own DNA.

BONE OF MY BONES and FLESH OF MY FLESH / 36

SPIRITUAL DNA

Stop to think about it. If you as a human were ill with something contagious, and you breathe upon someone else, the chances of that person carrying your bacteria would be highly probable. In the case of the Triune God, the breathing was intentional. The orifice for breathing, (the nostril) needed to be activated. The rest of the organs within the man, also needed to receive the oxygen required for living tissue. Each cell of the body needed activation. Even today, we do mouth to mouth resuscitation.

God wasn't just making a man, he was making someone who would represent him, in this new creation.

The inner man was infused with God's Spiritual DNA. Spiritual DNA cannot be seen by the naked eye. It cannot be discovered through chemistry. It cannot be distinguished by natural or artificial light. It is the essence of God. Only God can detect it, as it resonates with his frequency. It is like a tuning fork. It is detected by the Holy Spirit, whom by his own oscillation, can make the harmonic distinction in every human. Every human being ever born through man, has it. It is our identifier with the divine and will manifest in the true worship of spirit and truth. That manifestation, is the soul. It is the eternal living consciousness, preserved by God for his delight, in the transcendence of man, from physical death to eternal life, in Him.

> God wasn't just making a man, he was making someone who would represent him, in this new creation.

By having a divine nature, from God's spiritual DNA, man becomes a living soul. Within the earthen shell, would exist the potential of transcendence, between his created physical world and God's universe. The roadmap was embedded in man's DNA.

God's breath, was His signature upon and within the man. God deposited all of what man would need within and without, to manifest the same nature as God. Man was infused with God's DNA. As a man, to have the characteristics of God, meant that he owes his existence to the Triune God. Every cell of his body, was endowed with spiritual and divine instruction. The created body, would one day inhabit the Son of God. That body, in its physical form, was meant to understand and master all the emotions and feelings that were a part of God. As the first of his kind, man was perfect in every way. He needed to be! In him was the seed for all future generations of his kind. Just like every plant, tree, insect, animal above, below or in the water, had seeds to multiply and enrich God's new creation, so did the man. The Psalmist presents it this way:

> [Psalm 139:13-16 *"For You formed my inward parts; ...I will praise you, for I am fearfully and wonderfully made; ...My frame was not hidden from you, when I was made in secret, and skillfully wrought in the lowest parts of the earth. Your eyes saw my substance, being yet unformed. And in your book they all were written, the days fashioned for me, when as yet there were none of them".*]

The third phrase in Genesis 2:7 - <u>*man became a living soul.*</u>

> God's breath, was His signature upon and within the man. God deposited all of what man would need within and without, to manifest the same nature as God.

As I stated before, God deposited all of what man would need, within and without, to manifest the same nature as God. Every cell of his body, was endowed with spiritual and divine instruction. As the man was instructed and taught by the Creator, in connection with learning and storage of all information, the brain became the storehouse of this spiritual, divine and now, practical knowledge, of the earthly kingdom man was about to inherit.

BONE OF MY BONES and FLESH OF MY FLESH

UNDERSTANDING RELATIONSHIP

Man's direct influence with God as his teacher, presented the divine model for father/son relationship. The rest of nature, took note, about this relationship. The man, was being prepared for becoming Lord of the created universe. The Father was making sure, that his son, understood the nature of responsibility in love and harmony, for all things created. The man was introduced to the Triune God's other servants; the Cherubim, Seraphim, Archangels and Angels.

The man was trained in all aspects of the sciences. He needed to know about language and communication, light, dark, the seasons, time, plants, animals, music, art, colors, the constellations, respect for his Creator and all other life forms. The image of God, was imprinted every day, by the actions and behavioral patterns of God himself. The lifestyle of responsibility, was etched in man's intellect and his soul. It was presented in love and never in fear. Truth, was commonplace, every day of existence. There was transparency between the Triune God and the Man. There was nothing to hide.

GOD THE GARDENER

[*Genesis 2:8 "And <u>the LORD God planted a garden</u> eastward in Eden; and <u>there he put the man whom he had formed</u>".*]

How often in sermons or teachings has this verse been overlooked for the obvious? The Triune God plants a garden!

It may seem insignificant to many, but I find it interesting that of all places in the Bible, it is in Genesis that God becomes a gardener. Even before giving man full dominion over the new created universe, God plants a garden. Why?

We have been presented in our Christian life, with an image of this omnipotent Triune God that just seems to sit on his throne, like the top executive of a corporation, and all he does is listen to our prayers and orders the angels around, to execute his orders. Yet, here he is, with a hands on approach. The lesson being taught, cannot be overlooked. God is a doer! God has been working from the beginning. It is honorable and good for man, to understand that work, is a part of life. A model for the man. A reference point, about planting and taking care of the planet we were given, as an inheritance through the man.

In my imagination, I picture God thinking about his garden. Should it be a flower garden? Should it be a vegetable garden? What kind of garden? What purpose would it serve? He thinks about the location. It requires good soil, water, sunlight, and the best plants for the garden. Being God, he would have thought about every condition and situation for his garden.

> God is a doer! God has been working from the beginning. It is honorable and good for man, to understand that work, is a part of life.

The purpose for the garden, would have been a micro world for the man to learn and appreciate the ecological biosphere, of which later, he would be Lord of. Man would have been taught on the process of irrigation, photosynthesis, pollination, vines, bushes, flowers and trees. Man would learn about weather patterns and how they affect plant and animal life; how seeds were necessary in order to propagate the species; what plants were good for healing and for seasoning food. Man would learn about encroachment by other plants such as weeds, thistles and thorny bushes. He would need to know about support for fruit bearing trees and plants and how to control the plants from overtaking the place of others.

In this garden, man would learn about the perfect symbiosis of plants, insects and the interaction of other animal life, which depended from its care and maintenance. Endless lessons that would be required, to take care of a planet and beyond. The main lesson was, that the planet would provide man with anything needed to sustain his life, but he needed to work it. Once man understood the responsibility of working the garden, God tells him [Genesis 2:16 *"You are free to eat from any tree in the garden".*]. It was as if to say, you must work in order to eat and sustain the temple that encases your soul.

And God had his perfect garden. I'm sure he would go to it every day and check on the plant and animal life. He would speak with the plants. He would speak with the animals. He would rejoice in all the beautiful flowers and their vibrant colors. With each season, there would be a constant change in color, new life. He would meditate on how this garden would eventually propagate throughout the planet with man guiding it, according to the Master Plan. What a joy to eventually have man and his help meet, walk around the garden; what great conversations and learning sessions would take place; what questions would the man choose to ask? What would happen when man would see his first child? What an exciting time!

God was looking forward to sharing his garden and its benefits with the man. This garden would be the model for the eventual communion between the natural man and the eternal God. It would be the legacy of God for his own Son. It would be paradise. God placed the man he formed in the Garden.

> [Genesis 2:15 *"And the LORD God took the man, and put him into the Garden of Eden to dress it and to keep it."*]

BONE OF MY BONES and FLESH OF MY FLESH / 46

WHAT'S IN A NAME?

[*Genesis 2:19 "And out of the ground <u>the LORD God formed every beast of the field, and every fowl of the air; and brought them unto Adam to see what he would call them</u>: and whatsoever Adam called every living creature, that was the name thereof."*]

The man was created. He was placed in the garden. Now, we have an interesting event which seems to be out of context in the narrative, because God brings the animals to man, to name them, only to be followed by an expression of *"It is not good for man to be alone."*

What would be the purpose of God bringing the animals to man, in order to name them? Shouldn't it be fair that man have a name as well?

God called things into existence by naming them. From this, we can determine that naming belongs to the same act as creating. We do that today, to any creative idea or object that we forge. Naming, gives the name giver, authority over the receiver of the name.

In the English interpretation of the Bible, we pick up the name of the man, as Adam. The name, seems to be a derivative of the Hebrew word for earth. The word for earth is *'adamah (ad-aw-mah)*. Just from looking at the spelling of the word you can see the name *'adam'* within its letters. That is why, in some translations of the Bible, in *Genesis 1:27* it would read *"let us make man or Adam"*, into our own image. The applied name, was to be for man, a reference in remembering his origins. As in the case of dust, man would be reminded about how the physical body would return to the dust, the applied name of Adam, would remind him of what he had in common, with the rest of the created universe. His physical body was one with the earth. Plants and animals, all shared in the same symbiotic relationship. Adam's important difference was, that within him, he carried the divine DNA and a spiritual destiny of transcendence, beyond the life of plants and animals: his soul.

> God called things into existence by naming them.
> From this, we can determine that naming belongs to
> the same act as creating.

Once again, the Triunity's collective reasoning, foresaw the eventual devastation of the planet through sin nature and prepared ahead of time, its redemption and restoration. How so? In having made man from the earth and giving him the name of Adam, it made him Lord of the new creation, it made him its ally, its care taker. It gave him the inherent right, of title to the land. He came from it, he was one with it. Anything which happened to the man, happened to the earth. If man was good, the earth was good. If man was corrupt, the earth would be corrupted. Only man, could redeem and restore the planet.

Natural man, once corrupt, would not have the power to redeem or restore the planet. The Triunity having foreseen this situation, would eventually allow the "Second Adam" or the seed of Adam (meaning the Son of God, Christ Jesus), having a true divine nature, to come through Adam's descendants. Because Jesus would be truly divine and truly human, his sacrifice, would redeem humanity and the planet. Jesus alone, would be able to redeem and restore the planet, to the original garden state, as planned by God.

The naming of Adam, had to do with his dominion. By naming Adam, God had given him the power and dominion, over the created universe. Nature had to see for itself, that this man that was made from the earth, had the authority to define its destiny and purpose. God respected Adam's training and education as provided by him, to do what was right. It did not mean that Adam would rule alone. God would still be there to coach and mentor him. After all, there is no substitute for experience; God had all of it. All Adam had to do, was call on God the Father for assistance and he would be there. Here and now, by naming the animals, Adam ascertained his right to Lordship over God's newly created universe.

I feel there is another reason why God brings the animals so that Adam would name them. God is always preparing the way for us, even when we don't even think about it. That is his nature in love.

It used to be in past generations, that when husband and wife were expecting a child, if a man could not afford it, he would make a cradle for the expected child. It mattered not the gender. The parents would make provision beforehand for the child. As the child grew, the parents would always make provision for every need they could, based on their own experience. Even though the child, kept growing to be an adult. Parents made provisions for those situations in life that s/he may have not thought about.

God brought the animals to man, so that not only would he name them and give them purpose and destiny, as he himself had received, but to establish a rule of relationship. The naming of the animals, would give Adam authority over them. To this day, we are naming our pets. Whether living, artificial or even imaginary, we give our pets names. We give names to boats, cars, bicycles and a host of other inanimate things. Names are a form of ownership and relationship. It may be strange for me to say this, but no one of us really knows his true name. We know what we are called, (sometimes in not a nice way). Only God answered *"I am who I am"*. We see God and Jesus changing human names, so that the true destiny and purpose of the individual, would align with the divine call on their lives; i.e. Abram to Abraham, Jacob to Israel, Simon to Peter, Saul to Paul, etc.

In today's society, it seems that a name is given based on ancestry, or to honor some deity. We have lost relationship with God. We end up substituting God's destiny and purpose for the children, by substituting what we think is a pretty name. We tie down a child's ability to dream and grow, by not defining their God given destiny within their name. What a shame! Just think, if God had not changed the name of Abram to Abraham, we would never have been blessed as a nation. There is power in a name! There is relationship in a name. There is purpose and destiny in a name.

Adam, fulfills God's mandate for naming the animals. Mr. and Mrs. Horse now knew they were meant for each other; Mr. and Mrs. Goose took off in flight together; Mr. and Mrs. Whale swam off; Male and female was their gender respectively. It had to be that way, because without the God given way, they would not have been able to multiply and enrich the planet. The plants understood it. Now the animals understood it. Adam needed to understand it. Animals accepted their purpose and destiny, as well as their commitment to each other, for life.

BONE OF MY BONES and FLESH OF MY FLESH / 52

BEING ALONE IS NOT GOOD

[*Genesis 2:18 "And the LORD God said, It is not good that the man should be alone; I will make him a help meet for him".*]

In truth, Adam was never alone. He had the Triune God, the heavenly hosts, the animals, birds, fish and plants. Adam was alone in that, there was only one of his kind. Upon completion of his Master Plan for creation, Adam is placed as Lord of the new creation. There was no one else of his kind, to share this wonderful new world with. Social interaction, the appeal of the senses, communication, relationship with one's own kind, demanded another, such as Adam. In the mind of the Triune God, he had foreseen this moment. God's statement of being alone, was for the rest of creation, to understand that there would be others of Adam's kind.

God now knows, that Adam understands relationship and what it means to have a partner for life. Seeing that man is capable of taking dominion and stewardship of the created universe, he declares *"It is not good for man to be alone"*. A

Triune God, understood relationship within their self, from the beginning. He would not allow loneliness, to destroy his perfect creation. A culture of one, perishes within itself. God's purpose for creation, was the extension of the Triunity, into an ever living and evolving universe of life; an ever changing paradise of color, beauty, harmony and life in love, as in the existence of the Father, Son and Holy Spirit.

God sees that all he has created, is very good. Man can now perform the responsibility, for which he had been designed. God takes a rest on the seventh day, and blesses it.

God's rest was not a PTO (Paid Time Off) day; neither was it a vacation day. It was a lesson for man. If you work, you must rest. Your physical body needs to recuperate from daily activity, and the mind, needs a still atmosphere for processing. Plants and animals understood it and man needed to understand it. So, God sets the example. Such a wise father!

God's rest, also represented an eternal time of rest. When man's life ended, there would be a rest. The land needed to rest. Rest is a blessing from God. That is why the seventh day was blessed. It became a symbol of transcendence. It paved the way for a new beginning; a fresh start; fresh ideas; a new perspective. Without rest, degradation comes into play. God would never set a bad example for his creation. Rest gave God, the opportunity for reflection and quiet supervision. Man would run the show, but God was still in sovereign control.

A PROMISE OF HELP

[Genesis 2:18 *"The LORD God said, "It is not good for the man to be alone. I will make a helper suitable for him."*]

Adam was unique. He was the first. Adam was made by God, for God. Adam had no "mother", as we know it. All references he had of what a mother should be, was demonstrated by the Triunity. There really was no gender influence, because there wasn't one. That, would come later.

The Master Plan, called for Adam to be properly prepared in every aspect of being Lord. As God had been the father and the Holy Spirit the mother, fatherhood and motherhood, would eventually come through Adam.

The Triune God, saw firsthand, what Adam could do. With God's mentoring, he was able to take care of the garden. He was able to care for the animals. He understood time, seasons, relationships, respect, love, authority and the value of life. However, there was one thing that Adam needed to learn, that would be his crowning achievement. He needed to learn, that being Lord and steward of this new creation, wasn't a job for one man. He was not God. Adam needed to know about cooperation, intimacy, family, being a husband, being a father, being a priest and being a role model, for the generations that were yet to be born.

For the lessons needed to be learned by Adam in his next phase of development, the Triune God declares that *"it is not good for the man to be alone"*.

As I read this verse and compared it to *Genesis 1:26*, I noticed the grammatical construction difference between these two verses. In that first verse, it states *"let us make"*. It was the collective essence of the Triunity, which needed to be in agreement, for the creation of the man. By contrast, in the verse we are discussing (*Genesis 2:18*), the statement reads *"I will make a helper"*. I asked the Holy Spirit, why such a marked distinction, in the declaration of the statement? He answered me by saying: *"Because I wanted to be the Father of the Bride."* I was humbled, amazed and privileged to have received such revelation.

It made perfectly good sense. The Triune God was seeing the future from his standpoint. Just as in making the body for man, he was looking to the future habitation of his Son, God was looking to the future representation of the bride, the church, for his Son. Isn't God amazing and awesome!

God wanted to give Adam a helper, as his companion. God was not about to create another being for Adam. All that God had created, he called GOOD! Adam had come from the will of God, by design and purpose. His reference of identity was "I am from God" or "I come, I exists because he made me".

God was about to do something in the life of Adam, that would put creation at a personal level. As he was made by God, now God was going to make him a helper that came from him (Adam).

Adam had all that God needed to make his helper. By taking something from Adam, God knew that man would always feel incomplete, because something was missing from him. When you miss something, you will seek it, you will look for it. You will not be complete, until you find it. Just as Adam had come from God, now his help meet, would come from him.

In the process of preparing Adam's helper, God would take from Adam what was necessary, for him to physically, emotionally and intellectually understand the relationship, of the emotional, physical and intellectual needs of his helper. How would man understand this relationship? Because the helper, was an internal and integral part, of who he was as a man.

Man's understanding of relationship, prepared the way for Jesus and the church. The church is a part of Jesus. He gave birth to it. That is why, all relationship of God's children to the church, has its foundation in family. Everything that man has done, to break up the family, takes away from our relationship to God the Father, Jesus and the church.

BONE OF MY BONES and FLESH OF MY FLESH / 58

A SURGICAL PROCEDURE BY DR. GOD

[*Genesis 2:21 "So the LORD God caused the man to fall into a deep sleep; and while he was sleeping, he took one of the man's ribs and closed up the place with flesh. 22 Then the LORD God made a woman from the rib he had taken out of the man, and he brought her to the man."*]

God understands pain. He is the author of this uncomfortable feeling, in the life of man. This, should not come as a shock to anyone. When we were created, every feeling in our being, was placed there by God for a reason. You may say "well, I could have done without pain!" That being the case, you would have missed out on happiness. For every negative feeling, there is an opposite and positive feeling. The ones you cultivate the most, are the ones that reveal to people, your nature and character. Without the Triunity to assist in the management of these feelings, man by himself, would not be able to understand the different shades of their manifestation. For this reason, man will always need God at his side. The uncontrollable outburst of any emotion, puts the man's life and the life of others, in danger. God put the chemistry in our bodies and through His DNA, gave it the proper instructions, stored in our brain for the required dosage necessary, to procure a balanced result.

Having such understanding of feelings, God places man in a deep sleep, in order to continue with the next process of man's development. Adam, was about to receive a gift from God. [*James 1:17 "Every good gift and every perfect gift is from above, coming down from the Father of lights, with whom can be no variation, neither shadow that is cast by turning."*] I understand this deep sleep, as a patient about to undergo surgery. The physician and the family, prefer that the patient is, as comfortable as possible, in a very painful experience. In the case of Adam, it was the love, grace and mercy of God, which accounted for being placed in an anesthetic state. All together alive, but not participating in the process of his carnal pain.

When God undertakes this procedure, it is very symbolic. In a sense, the man is about to give birth to his wife, with the assistance from God. We might exaggerate this metaphor, by bringing to mind the epidural anesthetic given to a woman, before going into labor. The man is alive, in a deep sleep and God is about to make an incision over the rib cage, and not subject man to pain.

There have been many stories as to why God chose the rib bone to make Adam's help meet, but for the moment, I will reveal what the Holy Spirit has placed in my heart. God extracts the rib and seals the flesh back up again.

The Bible does not give details, as to what rib, whether it was from the left, or from the right rib cage. The Scriptures don't even make mention, whether it was from the lower, and upper or middle rib cage. If we even inspect the man, we can't even seem to find any bones missing from the rib cage. So what is the importance of the bone?

I am going to be over simplistic in my explanation, because anatomy, is best left in the hands of the professionals who can explain the details, better that I ever could. The bone marrow, is the place where the cellular elements of the blood are produced. It is the source for the treatment, of cancer cells and other human conditions. I believe God used the rib, in order to obtain Adam's DNA and make his help meet. There were no other humans. Adam was the first. Adam's help meet, had to be his perfect compliment. God knew, that the best way to make that happen, was to take from Adam's own gene pool. The difference in gender, needed to be established, and in drawing from man's DNA, God makes it happen.

As the first man, all the elements of reproduction, were in Adam's gene pool. The XX chromosome, was a part of him. In the making of the help meet God transfer the XX to the female, by taking a part of the man's XX chromosome, and making it XY. (Man does not give up the rib, he provides the content of the rib or the bone marrow, in order for God, to make his help meet.) In the divine, as well as in human nature, the man would make the determination, about the sex of the child. However, man cannot do it alone. It takes the woman, to contribute one of her X genes and the sex is determined. As God determined to make man first and then the help meet. So in the natural, it is the man through his contribution of an X or Y gene, to the woman's contribution of her X gene, which determines the sex of the child.

In summary, God was not about to create another being for Adam. All that God had created he called GOOD! Adam had all the good that God needed, to make his helper. By taking something from Adam, God knew, that man would always feel incomplete, because something was missing from him. When you miss something, you will seek it, you will look for it. You will not be complete, until you find it.

In the process of preparing Adam's helper, God took from Adam, what was necessary for him to physically, emotionally and intellectually understand this new relationship. How would man understand this relationship? Because the helper, was an internal and integral part of who he was as a man.

By taking Adam's rib, God "extracts" from the bone marrow in the rib, the required chromosome information that was necessary, to meet the helper Adam required. Man no longer required the "XX" gene. God takes it and makes it "XY". He then introduces the "XX" chromosome to the helper. Man is now incomplete without his helper. He will always need his helper. The woman becomes the complement of the man.

Man is not missing a rib. He is missing part of his DNA which is now in woman. Now he is able to complete the mandate with his helper to multiply and enrich the earth.

A WOMAN IN THE MAKING

To have a destiny, is to have a future; to have a goal; to know where you are headed. It means you have purpose.

This, was the role of the help meet. She was not just some appendage to the man. This would not be her role in this new creation. The Triune God does not bring anything into existence, without a complete understanding of the role and function for its being. Before Adam called her Woman, God knew how the man would designate the help meet. Every conceivable notion of the man's need, God took into consideration, in the making of the woman. She was made perfect for Adam.

Her anatomy, charm, poise, intelligence, wisdom, awareness of self and every good grace and gift was bestowed on Adam's helper. She was not made a slave or a servant who comes only when requested. As well as God had made and knew Adam, so his helper was endowed to be his support. Her thoughts and actions, were meant to complement Adam's role in the stewardship, of the

Natural Kingdom, to whom he was made Lord.

The Triunity saw her role, not just as a woman who was brought into existence from the man. Just as the man would be a representation of the person of Jesus, the woman would become the representation for the church, the bride of Christ.

> As well as God had made and knew Adam, so his helper was endowed to be his support.

It is the woman, who carries the legacy of the man. Within the woman, God made sure, that there was a place for the seed of man to take hold and grow. [*Genesis 1:28 ..."Be fruitful and increase in number; fill the earth and subdue it."*] God's mandate for the couple was clear. Be fruitful and multiply. Neither could do it, without the other. Even though they were separate lives, they would only survive as one. A man who despises his helper, puts an end to his own existence; puts an end to his own legacy. To think of a woman, only for the selfish act of propagating his seed, man reduces his divine calling to an animalistic nature, of survival of the species.

> God's mandate for the couple was clear. Be fruitful and multiply. Neither could do it, without the other. Even though they were separate lives, they would only survive as one.

God created the animals first, so that man could become the Lord over all creation. Man defined the destiny of the animals, by giving them a name. To this day, they have been loyal to their purpose and destiny. The animal's obedience to God, gave them priority in God's saving grace, when He destroyed the planet with water. It was the animals, who entered into the ark first. When man thinks of his own need first and does not follow God's Master Plan, he is no longer representing the image of God. Man becomes as an animal. In the book of Daniel, is a description of a man turned animal. [*Daniel 4:33 "Immediately what had been said about Nebuchadnezzar was fulfilled. He was driven away from people and ate grass like cattle. His body was drenched with the dew of heaven until his hair grew like the feathers of an eagle and his nails like the claws of a bird."*] God's men are not animals, they are to be Lords of this creation. Their wives are to be respected and admired, for being their help, in carrying the legacy for which they were destined.

Woman has been the chosen vessel, for the salvation of humanity. [*Genesis 3:20 "Adam named his wife Eve, because she would become the mother of all the living."*]

Throughout history, woman has been revered and in some cultures, she is worshiped like a god. She has represented virtues, such as truth, wisdom and justice in the female form. Still In some cultures, she is but a piece of flesh, a slave, a commodity to be bought, sold or traded. She has been the spoils of war, the treasure of kings or a warm blanket for a cold blooded male. How disastrous! Men have not welcomed the helper, for who or what she is.

Women, take heart. The God that formed you, saw the potential in you, to bring forth the salvation of humanity.

You who have been betrayed, despised, bought, sold, traded, beaten, raped, discarded and unappreciated, your Father in heaven, has redeemed you and made you worthy, of carrying his seed: his Son, for the salvation of humanity. Without you, there would be no Savior, no redemption, no restoration, no grace, no favor and no man, to fulfill the mandate. Without you, there is no next generation.

From the moment she was formed, Eve understood the relationship, Adam had with God. She understood her own relationship with God, and the relationship of God with them. Woman had, and has, an insatiable hunger for knowledge. Eve understood what "helper" meant. She wanted to make sure that she understood things, in order to make Adam's position and role with this new creation, meet the approval of her Father. Even today, we say that behind every successful man, there is a woman.

Eve's desire for knowledge, became her Achilles' heel. It provided the right condition for the serpent's intriguing dialog, which prompted a disobedient course of action. This was the open door, the prince of this world needed [*Ephesians 2:2 "…the prince of the power of the air, the spirit who now works in the sons of disobedience…"*], to take over the new creation, and become its ruler. The enemy knew, if he attacked now, before Adam's generations were born, the venom of sin, which would be introduced, would be carried throughout generations and he, would reign over sin forever. Talk about a deceiver!!! [*1Timothy 2:14 "And Adam was not the one deceived; it was the woman who was deceived and became a sinner."*]

Let me interject, that there is nothing wrong with seeking knowledge. It is a gift from God. [*Colossians 3:10 "...put on the new man who is renewed in knowledge according to the image of Him who created him"*] It is when we seek knowledge from the wrong sources, that we get lies, half-truths and corrupted wisdom, tempting us, to second guess ourselves and ending up with a weak faith, that leaves gaping holes to our spiritual defenses. [*1 Corinthians 15:34 "Awake to righteousness, and do not sin; for some do not have the knowledge of God".*]

It seems that the woman is always "pushing" the man, to get things done. Man calls this "nagging". But disgruntled as the man may be, he eventually sees it her way, if he is aligned with God. God did not place woman in the role of policing man. However, God gave woman the grace and techniques, for the subtle urging of man, to accomplish his God given destiny. The fulfillment of man's destiny, assures the woman of her place in the kingdom. With man's true helper at his side, there is nothing the two can't accomplish together. [*Matthew 18:20 "For where two or three are gathered together in my name, there am I in the midst of them."*]

Eve was graced with a more sensitive spirit in the natural, than Adam. This was not favoritism, it was just God's favor. She would be the one to carry within her, for a gestation period of approximately 40 weeks, the seed of man, into its full term. The sensorial acuteness of the woman, had to be superior to man. New life, takes a lot of nurturing. Any woman will tell you that having a baby, is a life changing experience. I am not qualified, to detail the changes that a woman goes through, in the process of child bearing. That is someone else's story. My spirit understands it. My mind just can't begin, to put it into words.

This extreme sensitivity, is coupled to woman's destiny, as foreshadowing the church. When a woman is pregnant, her life is full of expectations for this new life. This was part of her endowment from God, so that she could begin praying and interceding for this new life. She needed to present man, with the fruits of her labor. She lovingly and without reservation, gave to the seed of man, all the nutrients of her own life, so that the legacy and promise of eternal life, promised by God to man, would be fulfilled. If the child dies; is still born, the woman will always feel it more deeply, than man. She will grieve longer and never forget, about the life that could have been.

As a man, you would ask or should ask, why does the woman go through such mourning? The Holy Spirit tells me, that it is because, in the course of her destiny, a still born child, carries with it, her inability to fulfill God's mandate. Her soul, has to deal with, a life that could have made the difference in the purposes of God's Master Plan and now as the mom, she feels responsible that the life, did not come to fruition. She feels, there is something wrong with her. What if she can't fulfill her role as helper to the man? What is he going to think? She thinks: Is he going to reject me, because I can't bring his legacy into the world? It haunts her in the perpetual why? For a woman, every life is precious, because from the moment it stirred in her body, love, the greatest of emotions, invaded her body and soul with possibilities. The very principle of faith, was unfurling every day. The substance of things hoped for, would soon be manifested!

The very feelings a woman goes through, are the very feelings or should be the very feelings, of the church. They are one in the same. Menstruation in the woman, is a sign of her fertility. Menstruation in the church, is preparation for revival. Get rid of the old blood that is ineffective, and infuse it with new life, for its destiny as the bride of Jesus. There is celebration in heaven, each time a new believer comes into the church body; as such there are festivities, when a new baby comes into the family. There is nurturing, training, education and preparation for that child to become an adult and take its place in society. There is need for food, language, human interaction, social behavior and so much more. The same applies to the church. Just as the extended family comes to the aid of a new born, the church body, comes to the aid of a new believer.

It is the mother, who nurtures the relationship between the children and the father. When the father is present, the home feels secure. So, the presence of the Father is important to the church. The presence of both parents in the harmony of God, provides, security, stability and a model for the children. The tenderness demonstrated by the father to his wife, will impress the image upon his daughter, of the loving husband, she will seek one day. It is the same of the son, as he looks to mom, for the image of the wife he will one day marry. The reverse of these conditions, also applies. Lack of tenderness, abusiveness of any kind, or lack of any love language, will impact the next generation with the same, or more violent actions.

In the case of the absent father, there is much that the children will never learn, and therefore, their generation will be lacking. Theirs, will be a generation of dysfunction. It will be, a discovery based relationship. Without the guidance of the Holy Spirit, if and when it is sought, restoration will or will not happen, for that next generation, from an absentee father or mother.

This is why God the Father, is always present to anyone who seeks Him. There is no need for an ancestry or Google searches. [*Matthew 7:7 "Ask, and it shall be given you; seek, and ye shall find; knock, and it shall be opened unto you…"*] As if that were not enough, He sent his only begotten Son, our big brother, so that we would not be bullied, or pushed around.

The church also has a responsibility, to model the relationship, between its members and the Triune Father. There is much nurturing and disciplining of a new believer, in order for him or her to fulfill the five-fold ministry responsibilities, in the church body. In as much as there is gift giving in the natural, there is much gift giving, in the spiritual. As there is pain and sorrow in the loss of a baby, so there is pain and sorrow, in the church body, when it loses one of its members, for some unexpected reason.

The parallels are formidable. That was the reason, why God decided to be the Father of the Bride. It will be He, who will present the bride to his Son. The Bible was written in the East. The culture, is embedded within Scripture. In Jewish culture, the marriage is arranged from birth, by the parents. They follow the pattern set up by God. From the beginning, man's helper would be the bride presented by God. From the beginning, God had prepared his only Son to receive the bride; the church. That marriage, was arranged in heaven, and is soon to be celebrated at the wedding feast of the Lamb, when the Master Plan designed by the Triunity, is fulfilled. Glorious!

The woman that trusts in God, can accept more readily, the course of actions in her life, if she is dedicated to Him. Her spirit, in alignment with the Holy Spirit, will bear witness, in love and wisdom that God's will has been done, on earth as it has in heaven.

BONE OF MY BONES and FLESH OF MY FLESH / 72

BONE OF MY BONE AND FLESH OF MY FLESH

[*Genesis 2:23 "The man said, "This is now bone of my bones and flesh of my flesh; she shall be called 'woman,' for she was taken out of man."*]

God fulfilled His promise to man. Man would no longer be alone. God the Father had formed a bride for Adam. She would be his helper. Adam spoke. He didn't just think about it, as a fleeting thought of what was to be. He confessed it out loud before God, the heavenly hosts and the new creation. This was to be woman, because she came from the "womb" of man.

As Adam had come from God, his help meet came from him. Adam spoke to his destiny; to the future of his children and their children. Adam spoke to humanity's future, as God would speak to the future church.

Why did Adam say *"bone of my bone"*? I believe, there is a two part answer to the question. The first part, was a conscious awareness to the fact, that Adams own creation, was half divine and hand half flesh. The second part, comes from an awareness of the fact, that his help meet, came from his inside, as he had come from the inside image of God. Adam's mention of the bones, is a reference point to the structural support form, of the being. In other words without a structure - a support - flesh would just be a mass of matter, without function.

Bone of my bone spoke to the fact, that the woman wasn't just a "blob". She had structure. She could stand, move, reach out, sit, climb, and lay down, all on her own. Structure, speaks of foundation. It speaks of government. It speaks of order. It speaks of equality.

Adam took a good, close look, at the woman God gave him. I imagine, he went by the water and took a look at the reflection of himself and compared what he saw, with the gift that was before him. He noticed the similarities and the differences. He looked at hands and feet, the face, the body, the hair, the eyes and the graceful lines. He looked from top to bottom, front to back, as he walked around her. He gently touched her, felt the warmth of her body, felt the texture of her hair. At the same time, the woman did the same thing. She looked at Adam and studied him. The two, were as if on a rotating pedestal, absorbing all the details of each other. There was no shame, as they stared at each other. There was only transparency.

There was something else. Adam had never experienced this before. As close as he was with the Triune God, this exuberance, was different. It was powerful. It was wonderful, alluring and mystical. There was contentment within the man. He looked to God, as if to say "What is this strange sensation that has come over me?" The Almighty beamed like the sun, and said "This is love, in its fullest expression! What you have begun to feel, is the same satisfaction we felt, when we created you. It will come to you and your helper, in different ways and expressions, in different stages, of your lives. This is our eternal gift to you and your generations". Adam then replies, *"she shall be called 'woman, for she was taken out of man."*

All of creation looked on, at the magnificence of God's gift to the Lord of this new creation. They subjected themselves in obedience, as requested of God.

Besides having form and structure, as in *"bone of my bone"*, Adam also commented: *"this is flesh of my flesh"*. Why make the distinction? Adam recognized, that his helper was not just another creation. She wasn't a part of any other thing, created by God. She, had been made from his own essence. He himself, had a direct connection, with the divine and the spiritual. Her connection with the divine, or spiritual, was indirect, through Adam but she, was flesh of his flesh. She was different, but at the same time, she was him. God had taken from Adam, not just structure and form, but his feelings, emotions, sensitivities, all that comprised his own flesh, to give him, the helper, with whom he would relate for the rest of his life. Adam, now had someone with whom he could talk, share his thought process, and explore new ideas. He could now begin to teach, what he had learned from God, to his own kind. They began to communicate about this wonderful Creator. As they faced each new day, they worshipped in thanksgiving, communion, fellowship and joy, the God that had brought them, into existence. They began to experience companionship and a fondness for each other. Being apart, was inconceivable. They had discovered relationship. Adam's flesh, had given birth to God's promise of a help meet. She was everything Adam needed, to complete God's Master Plan. They were given the mandate to *"go forth, multiply and enrich the planet."*

As man had been created from the earth, and all the components of his creation were in common with nature; flesh, spirit and soul, were now in unity on earth, as it is in heaven. God's image for man, now conformed. [*Ephesians 4:24 "And that ye put on the new man, which after God is created in righteousness and true holiness."*] [*Colossians 3:10 "...put on the new man, which is renewed in knowledge after the image of him that created him."*]

Righteousness, truth, wisdom and government, were ready to fulfill their function on earth, as his Creator had done in heaven. God steps back to being the provider for all life, and allows man, to supervise it. The fish in the sea, the birds in the sky and every living thing that walks or crawls on the earth, would honor man and man would honor God. [*1Corinthians 3:22, 23 "...the world, or life, or death, or things present, or things to come; all are yours; and ye are Christ's; and Christ is God's."*] [*Psalm 145:9-12 "The LORD is good to all: and his tender mercies are over all his works. All thy works shall praise thee, O LORD; and thy saints shall bless thee. They shall speak of the glory of thy kingdom, and talk of thy power; to make known to the sons of men his mighty acts, and the glorious majesty of his kingdom"*]. Everything God created was in fact good, but his greatest delight, is in the relationship with mankind.

God, now makes a statement for all generations. [*Genesis 2:24 "Therefore shall a man leave his father and his mother, and shall cleave unto his wife: and they shall be one flesh."*]

> Everything God created was in fact good, but his greatest delight, is in the relationship with mankind.

The basic premise for marriage, had now been established by God. Adam's declaration confirmed it. Bone of my bone and flesh of my flesh meant, that neither the man nor the woman, could live separated from each other. She, was his bone and flesh. She, was made for him. [*1 Corinthians 11:9-12 "Neither was the man created for the woman; but the woman for the man. ...Nevertheless neither is the man without the woman, neither the woman without the man, in the Lord. For as the woman is of the man, even so is the man also by the woman; but all things of God."*]

Whenever a man takes on the responsibility of marriage, he takes unto himself a wife, he fulfills the mandate from God himself. Notice that the Word says that the man, not the woman, leaves his father and mother. In a society that has turned its back on God, the reverse trend is happening. Women are leaving the father and the mother, to live with a man, who has not left his own mother and father.

When the divine model is not followed, failure in marriage, prevails.

A man, needs to provide for his help meet. She, was designed for him and not the other way around. We are not talking about some stranger. She is bone of your bone and flesh of your flesh. Mom and dad, have their own bone and flesh to worry about.

> Bone of my bone and flesh of my flesh meant, that neither the man nor the woman, could live separated from each other. She, was his bone and flesh. She, was made for him.

How can a man be responsible for a woman, when he has not willingly, opted to leave the house of his father and mother? He is not ready! Children need to grow up. They, need to take on their responsibility. They, have to define their own God given destiny. If the parents have done their job correctly, the children will have the required skills, by the time of adulthood, to realize themselves in the world. The parents should be there, as mentors and not meddlers. They are encouragers, of what is right and just. They are not discouragers, pinning one partner against the other. The parent's Christian lifestyle, should continue to set an example for the newer generation. The children must leave, their father and mother. This does not mean disrespect, on the part of the children. This does not mean abandonment, on the part of the parents. Let each take its rightful place in the world, with mutual respect and understanding. Each one teaching, coaching and mentoring, about the best of the gifts they have received from God. Family, forever shall be family. The closer the bonds are at home, the fonder the hearts become, when they are absent from each other. Family, is the first ministry.

Women take note. Ever since sin nature was introduced in the world, man is no longer the priest or governor, over his own life. Only godly men, living a true Christian lifestyle, will value the woman that God has for them. Beware the man, you have set your eyes upon!

Is this man an adult, or a child, in adult clothing?

Is he working; have a vocation; has a profession?
Is he responsible in his job?
Is he responsible in the management of his own affairs?
Does he mange, or know how to manage money?
How is his relationship with his mother and father?
Does he have a mother, living, deceased?
Does he have a father, living, deceased?
How well does he get along with his brothers and sisters?
Does he favor one brother or one sister, over the other?
Does he speak well of his family, friends, relatives, co-workers?
Is he a good steward of his time; punctual?
Does he have any pets?
How does he treat that pet?
Does, can, will he cook?
Does he know how to wash clothes?
Is he a good dresser?
Does he have a good sense of style?

Is he a good communicator?
Does he have good personal hygiene?
Is he from another country?
Are there cultural issues that must be explored?
How does he act or react, when you are around?
How does he present you, when you are with his friends?
How does he feel about owning a house?
How does he feel about children?
How many children?
Is he renting?
What can he offer you that you don't already have?
Does he have some type of addiction?
Does he like to put his life on the line?
Do you come first in his life?
Is he a believer in God and is he bearing testimony that Christ lives in him?
What do his friends male and female say about him?
Does he keep his word?
Is he a good listener?
What are his views on ministry regarding women?
How does he feel about a woman, with a calling from God?

You men who are reading this, the same criterion needs to be applied to the woman, whom you feel attracted to. Remember; the choice about your partner, is a lifetime contract. This is not a science experiment to see if it works. God is not in the business of experimenting. Everything he did, he did well! Adam was not presented with different types of women to choose from. God gave him exactly what he needed. If you are faithful, patient and seek the help from God, I guarantee, that he will supply you, with your true help meet.

We don't live in a perfect world any more. We need to see with God's eyes. Without him, your judgement will be based on outward appearance. With Him, you will see what is inside first, and then the outside will match the inside.

The man or the woman you choose as your partner, will be your husband or she may be your wife. He, will be the role model, for your daughter's eventual selection of a husband and she, will be the role model for the eventual wife, your son will marry. You will either bless, or curse your children. As you get older, ask yourself one question: Will my children and grandchildren want me around their home, when I get old? Prepare the way now, with God. Develop a great natural and spiritual relationship with your children.

BONE OF MY BONES and FLESH OF MY FLESH / 82

SHE SHALL BE CALLED EVE

[Genesis 3:20 "And Adam called his wife's name Eve; because she was the mother of all living."]

The progression of the creation story, has Triunity's specific timing, in the revelation of things, according to his divine plan. It is not until Genesis chapter 3, that we know the name of the helper, that Adam calls woman.

First, Adam defines her origin. She is called woman, because she came from man. Then, he defines her role and relationship, by giving her the name of Eve, meaning: life giver.

The Triune God, had put his Master Plan into action. Man, had been put in charge of this new creation. The promise of a helper, had been fulfilled. Man, was not alone. All of creation, was subjected under man's dominion, as the heavenly hosts witnessed the events, of the Master Plan. It was Adam's turn to take over. The scepter had been passed. God, would be the Lord over all of heaven and Adam, Lord of the earth, within God's heaven.

Adam's first act as Lord, is to name his helper. She, is now introduced as Eve, the giver of life. The first woman; the vessel by which God's purposes and man's destiny, would be fulfilled. The mother of mankind. The symbol for the bride of Jesus. Divinity and humanity, joined together according to the Master Plan. She, would be the first human matriarch. Adam, the first human patriarch. It was now that they could fulfill the mandate from God, to multiply and enrich the earth. [*Isaiah 46:10 "Declaring the end from the beginning, and from ancient times the things that are not yet done, saying, My counsel shall stand, and I will do all my pleasure."*]

HONORING THE WOMAN – A FORGOTTEN PERSPECTIVE

Any man, that seeks the blessing of a priest or of the church, for the purpose of marriage, should understand or needs to understand, the reason why he needs to honor that woman. From the very moment the thought enters his head, it is not by happenstance. It is in his spiritual DNA. The principles of honor, respect or reverence, do not come from a sinful man. It is the product of the gift of love. The Triunity placed it in the man from the beginning. It stems from a man that has a relationship with God and honors God. Respect begets respects.

A man needs to honor the woman because God does! From the beginning, God respected man enough, to make him a help meet, not from another body, not from another substance or element, she was made for him from him. Adam respected/honored God, who honored him, with woman. Adam's exclamation summed it up: this is bone of my bone and flesh of my flesh. From that day forward, anything that man would do for his body, he would do for his woman. If he repudiated his woman, he would be repudiating his own bone and flesh. Everything good, bad, or indifferent, that man would say or do to the woman, not only would he be insulting God, but he would be doing it to himself.

That is why God created the animals first, and then called man to name them, before giving him the help meet. Animals choose their mate for life. They understand the relationship. They understand the mandate to this day, to multiply and populate the planet. Animals get it! They protect the female, they provide food and shelter, they seek out a safe place for their offspring, they teach them how to be adults and how to fend and defend themselves. They take their God given responsibility, seriously. They honor God. Sometimes I think, that when God was about to destroy the world with water, He saved the animals first because they were obedient. They came when they were called.

> God respected man enough, to make him a help meet, not from another body, not from another substance or element, she was made for him from him.

A man needs to honor the woman because in doing so, it keeps him from becoming unkind, unfaithful, unhurting and unbecoming. Reciprocating these character traits, the woman blends in with the man. His understanding of her biology, respects the comparative weakness of her gender. Especially, during the time of birthing, there is great fatigue and hardship. Many sicknesses may prevail, as connected with child bearing. The man should treat the woman with greater respect and more regard. At that moment in life, she is fulfilling her God mandated purpose. She is fulfilling the legacy of the man: the mandate from God. To use and abuse women, for the sake of personal gratification, is not only selfish but it is sinful. The generational impact upon the family, for this egotistical attitude, is exponential. Any man, which carries on this kind of behavior, has lost his relationship with God and has no respect for himself or others.

Honoring the woman, goes beyond the intimacy and experience of self. Man needs to show esteem and affection for his woman, as he does for himself. She is bone of his bone and flesh of his flesh. Honor her before friends, family, in public places; support her and family, within the scope of what is just and righteous before God. Where she is incapable, or unskilled, provide for her needs. Look after her comfort and reputation. If you are gifted with wisdom and knowledge beyond hers, don't be offended by the little things. Humor her. Use your wisdom and knowledge to elevate her. Do not to demean or scold her, especially in public, or in the presence of family and friends. Remember, women as well, are coheirs with Christ, the same as man. You should wisely counsel, teach, encourage, motivate and uplift your helper. Your personal, physical or emotional stability, will be challenged somewhere in life, and you will reap what you have sown. This is to say, that at some point in your life, you may become sick, incapacitated, handicapped, limited in your obligation as husband, father, friend or companion. If you have not cultivated a positive relationship, with the woman you have chosen to be your wife, you will be alone. That is the place, God said that you should not be: alone! Woman, she is your companion in this pilgrimage.

Take it from me. I have traveled to several countries. I have traveled alone and accompanied by my wife. When she is there, we have conversations, reflections, she sees things and behaviors that I miss, she points out important things that I take for granted or have overlooked. Where my social skills may be lacking, she most graciously takes the lead.

You are not just honoring a woman. You are honoring your ministry partner. You are honoring your armor bearer. You are honoring your prayer warrior. You are honoring God. You are honoring your church in ministry. You are modeling the Christian lifestyle. You are modeling for your children and other couples. You are making a lifestyle statement: that being Christ centered, honors the Father that is in Heaven.

In the present state of humanity, as a man or woman, you may find yourself in a position, that you have a non-converted spouse. How does one deal with that? This is more of a reason, why you should honor that wo/man. S/he should see in you the goodness, grace and mercy of a loving God, a saving Christ and a manifestation of the gifts of the Holy Spirit. How else is s/he going to honor you, if s/he can't see the change God is doing in your life? S/he will be your first convert. How you honor your partner, will mean success or failure, in any aspect of ministry.

DISOBEDIENCE - THE INCEPTION OF SIN

The Triunity's Master Plan, predisposed one singularity – Obedience. Everything that God commanded, through speech or will, was complied with, under this one singularity. Creation, understood the Creator. It understood, that its existence, function, purpose and destiny, were tied in to its only demand: obedience.

In the beginning, obedience was a willful act of submission to the Creator out of love and gratitude, for existing. Every living thing, understood this underlying principle. In contemporary society, obedience is considered to be a sign of weakness, a slave mentality. It takes a lot more courage, determination, temperance, wisdom and patience to submit voluntarily, than to be a tyrant, dictator and a despot. Behold Jesus, the Son of God, and the best example of obedience: [*Philippians 2:8 "And being found in fashion as a man, he humbled himself, and became obedient unto death, even the death of the cross."*]

Before I digress from the present topic, I must remind my

beloved reader, about the omniscience and sovereignty of God. I speak now, through the authority of His Holy Spirit and not as myself.

God's sovereignty, by his own nature, gives him the authority to do as he wills and no one can question it. [*Hebrews 6: 13 "For when God made promise to Abraham, because he could swear by no greater, he swore by himself..."*] That is, because unless there is someone higher than He, with some other Master Plan, it has not revealed itself, since the era before mankind.

> God's sovereignty, by his own nature, gives him the authority to do as he wills and no one can question it.

Therefore, everything that eye has seen, ear has heard or thought that has entered into the mind of man, has come to be, by the will and work of the Triunity of God. In the book of Daniel, in the Old Testament, Nebuchadnezzar, a pagan Babylonian King, decreed... [*Daniel 3:29 "Therefore I make a decree, That every people, nation, and language, which speak anything amiss against the God of Shadrach, Meshach, and Abednego, shall be cut in pieces, and their houses shall be made a dunghill: because <u>there is no other God</u> that can deliver after this sort."*] (Author's emphasis.) By God's own words, when he is dealing with Pharaoh's disobedience, God says the following... [*Exodus 9:14 "For I will at this time send all my plagues upon thine heart, and upon thy servants, and upon thy people; that thou mayest know that <u>there is none like me in all the earth</u>."*]

God's omniscience means, that He knows everything. There is nothing that escapes Him. [*Colossians 2:3 "In whom are hid all the treasures of wisdom and knowledge."*] Should He fail, in any one aspect of His nature for existence, He would have to disqualify himself as a deity (God).

Humanity tends to question God about everything, when things don't go their way. Humanity is always looking to find fault and blame, simply because it is unable to either forgive itself or take responsibility for its own actions.

Today, the degree of disobedience in humanity, borders on the edge of blatant rebelliousness. Man does as he thinks and comes to varying conclusions about the existence of God. This is why, the Triune God continues to monitor and intervene, in the disobedience of mankind, so that order and not chaos, prevails in the Master Plan.

God gave one specific command to Adam. [*Genesis 2: 16-17 "And the LORD God commanded the man, saying, 'of every tree of the garden thou mayest freely eat: But of the tree of the knowledge of good and evil, thou shalt not eat of it: for in the day that thou eatest thereof thou shalt surely die.'"*]

There was no "either or", conditional language, in God's statement to Adam. Adam was free to eat from every tree in the garden including the tree of life. [*Genesis 2:9 "And out of the ground made Jehovah God to grow every tree that is pleasant to the sight, and good for food; the tree of life also in the midst of the garden, and the tree of the knowledge of good and evil."*] There was no choice; it was a sovereign command "...*of the tree of the knowledge of good and evil, you shall not eat of it..."*

Many may argue, that this was a test for Adam. God did not need to test Adam. He created Adam. He knew what Adam was capable of. In all of Adam's development, God had been Father, teacher, mentor, friend and companion. God would have educated Adam, on the two trees in the middle of the Garden.

He may have said something to the fact that the tree of life was for Adam's benefit. He may have said something like "Adam, you have been created from the dust of the earth. Every living thing has been made of the earth. In the course of time, you will age as will the animal life around you. They are not eternal beings like myself or the different ranking angels that I have created. This tree of life, has been created for your benefit. As you have children and they have children, and the animals begin to reproduce themselves; cuts, scrapes, sickness or other maladies may affect them. It will be your responsibility to care for your family. This tree of life, will sustain and prolong your life and health, and that of all your descendants".

Adam may have commented "You are God, you made me. Couldn't you heal me or my family if something were to happen to me?"

God may have answered something like "Adam, I created you to be Lord of this new creation. Your family will look up to you for answers, guidance, counseling and direction, about this world that I have created for you and your descendants. You will have to teach them about me. Teach them who I am. Let them know about our relationship; who are the angels what their function and purpose is. Keep in mind, that I am an eternal spirit. They will not see me with their human eyes. I will work through you, and by your example, they will know who, and what, I am. Also, keep in mind, that as your family and other families grow and develop, you may not always be there to impart wisdom and knowledge. If you teach them about us, they will develop trust. They will ask questions just as you have, and I will be there with answers or will send my angels, to minister and assist with their needs and wants."

In the ensuing conversation, Adam may have said "I understand now about the tree of life, but what about this tree you have called the *'the tree of the knowledge of good and evil?"*

God may have said "The fruit of that tree, develops a knowledge that at the present time, you are not ready to understand yet. I will decide when you are ready, and I will teach you about good and evil, just as I have taught you about everything else. For now, I forbid you to eat of that one tree."

The trust Adam had in God, was sufficient, and he obeyed without question.

BONE OF MY BONES and FLESH OF MY FLESH / 94

THE PERSONA OF SATAN - AGENT OF SIN

Chronologically speaking, the oldest book in the Bible is the book of Job. The first five books of the Bible; Genesis, Exodus, Numbers, Leviticus and Deuteronomy, are first in the compendium, because of the creation story; but the oldest according to historians, scholars and erudite, is the book of Job.

It is at the beginning of this book, that we are entreated to a meeting of the sons of God and the Lord himself. We are privy to the Lord God, in a conversation with a being called Satan.

> *[Job 1:6-12 "Now there was a day when the sons of God came to present themselves before the LORD, and Satan came also among them. And the LORD said unto Satan, Whence comest thou? Then Satan answered the LORD, and said, from going to and fro in the earth, and from walking up and down in it. And the LORD said unto Satan, Hast thou considered my servant Job, that there is none like him in the earth, a perfect and an upright man, one that feareth God, and escheweth evil? Then Satan answered the LORD, and*

> *said, doth Job fear God for nought? Hast not thou made a hedge about him, and about his house, and about all that he hath on every side? Thou hast blessed the work of his hands, and his substance is increased in the land. But put forth thine hand now, and touch all that he hath, and he will curse thee to thy face. And the LORD said unto Satan, Behold, all that he hath is in thy power; only upon himself put not forth thine hand. So Satan went forth from the presence of the LORD."]*

There is much to be said about these verses and it would be best covered in another book. So, we are going to focus on how this conversation fares, with the rest of our narrative.

As we delve into the Scripture, we see the Lord God, in the purpose of his business and inquiring of his heavenly creation, about the affairs of the Kingdom of Heaven. Scripture says that *"Satan came also among them."* Notice that it doesn't say, he was invited. It doesn't say that he was or wasn't welcomed. It does seem to indicate, that this persona - this being, has access to the throne of God.

In Hebrew the term, "Satan" or *"hassatan"*, means **adversary** and in Greek it is defined as **diablos**. In the English language it has been commonly translated as **the devil**. In alignment with these definitions, the Bible also defines this persona, in other ways.

In [*Revelation 12:9* he is defined as *"the **great dragon** was cast out, that **old serpent**, called **the Devil**, and **Satan**, which deceiveth the whole world."* *John 10:10* describes him as *"The **thief** cometh not, but for to steal, and to kill, and to destroy…"*

*Revelation 12:10 "...the **accuser** of our brethren is cast down, which accused them before our God day and night."*] Jesus addressing the Pharisees, refers to him as **the devil**, a **murderer**, a **liar** and **father of lies** in [*John 8:44 "Ye are of **your father the devil**, and the lusts of your father ye will do. He was **a murderer** from the beginning, and abode not in the truth, because there is no truth in him. When he speaketh a lie, he speaketh of his own: for **he is a liar**, and **the father of it**."*]

There are several things inferred, in the afore mentioned verses:

1. That God as Creator and Organizer of his Master Plan, likes to follow through, with his assignment of responsibilities.

2. That those to whom assignments are given by Him, are in fact, accountable for that responsibility.

3. That there is much work to be done in the Kingdom and God assigns the work to be done. Heaven is not a resort where you go to, be attended by angels, lie down on some cloud, and rest for eternity, with all the amenities you didn't have on earth.

4. That this being called Satan, apparently is known to the Sons of God and presents no threat. No one is alarmed and seems to accept, that this being, also reports to the Triune God on his endeavors. In other words, he, is also accountable to God.

5. That heaven is not a place of strife. Everyone knows their place. Regardless of rank, order or privilege,

everyone knows, that God takes charge for the implementation of justice, regardless of what form, shape or manner it may take.

Getting back to this persona of Satan. As sovereign over all creation, God asks him *"Whence comest thou?"* In other words, *"where are you coming from?"* As God, he would know where he was and what he was doing. The question and its answer, have a twofold purpose. One, for those who are present and do not have the power of omniscience, the opportunity presents itself, to hear the report. Two, for the truth, to be spoken before witnesses. The Lord does not permit lies, before the righteousness of His throne.

Satan, the adversary, responds: *"From going to and fro in the earth, and from walking up and down in it."* In other words, he says, without giving too much detail, *"from wandering here and there and walking about."* Apparently, this adversary's job is to wander and walk about the planet, to accuse humanity on the adverse or contrary things, that mankind does, in disobedience to God.

"Going to and fro in the earth", seems to imply, that he is aware of what the "surface dwellers" are doing and reporting on them, all the time. On the second part of his statement, *"walking up and down in it"*, seems to imply, that he, is connected with principalities "up" in the heavens as well as those that are in the occult, "down" parts of the earth.

With this brief report, which in a sense encompassed a lot, God responds to the adversary, in lieu of his constant accusations about humanity. He singles out one human being out of so many.

[*Job 1:8 "And the LORD said unto Satan, Hast thou considered my servant Job, that there is none like him in the earth, a perfect and an upright man, one that feareth God, and escheweth evil?"*]

This speaks volumes, about God's interest for humanity. He knows about the disobedience of humanity, as well as, the everyday life of the righteous people. You, may be one in a million, but you are important to Him, as a single human being. God knows you so well, that he is willing to place you in the hands of the adversary - Satan himself - in order to prove to him, that you, through your faith, are worthy of salvation above all accusations. [*2 Timothy 2:19"The Lord knoweth them that are his. And, Let everyone that nameth the name of Christ depart from iniquity."*] Satan's own fate, is sealed, for being disobedient and contrary to God's plans.

As well as God knows you, Satan, knows your strengths and weaknesses. He is fully aware, of who has the blessing of God and who does not. He is not concerned about the unfaithful, the disobedient and anyone who is contrary to the will of God, these are his friends and allies.

Job, was a rich cattle farmer. There was no other like him on the planet. He was perfect in making sure, that he always observed the laws of God. He would offer sacrifices for his children, to be sure that their sins, would not get in the way of their salvation. [As a reminder to our readers salvation came, only after Christ died on Calvary.] Job was upright. He was a just and fair man. He was a man of integrity. A man of his word. Job respected God and God did likewise.

Because of Job's personal testimony, before humanity in his own day, God had put a hedge of protection around him, his household, and everything he had at his side. This meant that Satan, had no way in, to attack.

God is not lazy. He works. He worked to create a universe. He worked to create a garden. He worked at creating all kinds of life. He works every day, to keep the world in harmony. He has even worked out his Master Plan, for the restoration of the planet, all of mankind and reconciling all things unto himself. That is why, God blessed the works of Job's hands and his cattle. Job, followed God's example.

My beloved reader, there are humongous rewards, for serving the Lord out of love, respect and obedience. In this description from Scripture, even the adversary, knows who the blessed of the Lord are. Notice that when God mentions Job by name, Satan doesn't ask who is he? Where does he live? Is he on F.B.? Can he receive text messages? Can he be tweeted? Satan knew who God was talking about, and had a file on Job, right down to God's brand of life insurance.

At this moment in our story, we read where Satan as the true adversary, lives up to his name, by asking God, to do his dirty work. He says to God: *"put forth thine hand now, and touch all that he hath, and he will curse thee to thy face."* In other words, take away all that you have given him, and watch how he will swear (bad mouth you) to your face.

God, is not in the business of taking away your blessings. That is the adversary's job. God may elect to allow you to be tested of Satan, for the sake of your testimony to him, and those around you. That's just for His Glory. It is you, as an individual, who will stand fast with God, to his testimony, or give up, your faith and witness for the Kingdom. God does not care about your possessions. He cares about your soul. That, is the part of you, which will celebrate in harmony, with the Triunity. That, is the part of you, which will integrate into eternity, for eternal service, in gratitude of His love for you.

God responds to Satan: *"Behold, all that he hath is in thy power; only upon himself put not forth thine hand. So Satan went forth from the presence of the LORD."* God granted permission. Note that Satan can't take things into his own hands, with God's children. Permission needs to be granted. It will be granted, if God is sure that you can overcome what the adversary has planned for you. However, this is not say that you don't need to take care, of your relationship with God. You have a responsibility, in relation to your salvation by Christ. [1 Peter 5:8 *"Be sober, be vigilant; because your adversary the devil, as a roaring lion, walketh about, seeking whom he may devour:"*]

Satan, was granted permission to attack all of Job's possessions, but not the man. The adversary wasted no time and left the presence of God. He attacked without mercy. He took everything Job had, even his children.

So, how did Job take this? [Job 1:20 *"Job arose, and rent his mantle, and shaved his head, and fell down upon the ground, and worshipped…"*] Job stood up. He took it like a man! He grieved tore his mantle, shaved his head and went down on all four, with his face to the ground. In verse 21 he sums it up. [*Job 1:21 "Naked came I out of my mother's womb, and naked shall I return thither: the LORD gave, and the LORD hath taken away; blessed be the name of the LORD."*]

The Bible sums it up this way: [*Job 1:22 "In all this Job sinned not, nor charged God foolishly."*] Job did not curse God! Satan was proved wrong! What would you have done, if you lost your farm, your workers, your cattle, your finances, your 10 children? Would you still be able to praise God?

Satan as Adversary, does his job very well. He did not give up on Job. In the second chapter of the book of Job, he is back again. He figures that since he couldn't touch the man, he would confront God once again to prove Him wrong. [*Job 2:4 "Satan answered the LORD, and said, Skin for skin, yea, all that a man hath will he give for his life."*] He says to God, that when it comes to saving his own skin, man will do anything, to save his life.

Talk about adding insult to injury. Job had not yet recovered from the first trial, only to face another, more personal and intimate one.

Satan goes even further. Once again, he requests that God, hurt man in his bone and flesh. Doing this, Job was going to curse (bad mouth), God to his face. [*Job 2:5 "put forth thine hand now, and touch his bone and his flesh, and he will curse thee to thy face."*]

Again, God grants permission for the adversary to attack his body, but with one condition. Satan could not attack his life. [Job 2:6 *"the LORD said unto Satan, Behold, he is in thine hand; but save his life."*]

Satan was happy. He got his wish. He would make living in the bone and flesh, as painful as possible for Job. He was sure, that this was the way, for man to renounce God. From head to toe, Satan attacked Job with sore boils. This may have been a form of smallpox. This produces sores and boils that irritate the flesh, itches, gives you fever and each pock, tends to enflame and suppurate. It creates such despair, that you want to scratch all your body at once, to find some relief from the itch.

When I first came to U.S.A. as a child, I was struck with a severe case of chicken pox. It was so bad, I was quarantined in the house and was not able to go to school, until cleared by a physician. I can relate first hand, with a similar situation, to what Job was going through. I was fortunate to have doctors, and nurses, to treat my fever from within. My mom would treat my body with calamine, in order to soothe the itching. I was nine years old and I still carry the scars on my body, to prove having gone through the ordeal.

Job did not have the benefits of a doctor, nurse, or a first aid kit. There were no dogs to lick his wounds, as in the case of Lazarus. He preferred to sit in the ashes, as this may have helped, in soaking up the suppuration. He used a piece of pottery, in order to scrape the areas that itched the most. He must have been so bad, that his body, would have smelled of rotting flesh. His wife came by to see him and she even said: 'curse your God and die.' This was not

Hollywood: once the filming is done, you can take off the makeup. This was suffering and torture at its finest, as only the one called Satan, could scheme up, in order for this man to curse God. If Job cursed God, Satan would have proved God wrong, but Job kept his mouth from sinning against God (verse 10). [*Job 42:12 "So the LORD blessed the latter end of Job more than his beginning."*]

My friend, my brothers and sisters in Christ: Mankind has this question: why do bad things happen to good people? The answer is read the book of Job. We are never exempt, from God's sovereignty. [*James 1:12 "Blessed is the man that endureth temptation: for when he is tried, he shall receive the crown of life, which the Lord hath promised to them that love him."*]

THE AGENT OF SIN STRATEGIZES AGAINST GOD AND THE FUTURE OF HUMANITY

In Job Chapter 2 and verse 5, Satan uses terminology quoted by Adam: *'bone and flesh'*. He uses it, in the same order as Adam. *"...Touch his bone and his flesh, and he will curse thee to thy face."* This, leads us back to our main departure point and title of this book Bone of my Bone and Flesh of my Flesh.

As we follow the sequence of events in Chapter 2, of the book of Genesis, God creates man, commands him to eat freely of every fruit of every tree in the garden, but of the tree of knowledge of good and evil, he should not eat, because he would surely die.

God's plan, involved a family after his own heart, as the Triunity. Man, was just the beginning of the family unit. God reviews the Master Plan and considers his next step of creation, to which he exclaims: *"It is not good for the man to be alone. I will make him a help meet."* In other words, I will make him one of his own kind. However, before he creates the help meet, he decides to create every beast of the field and every fowl of the air, to see how the man was going to name them. After this, he puts the man to sleep and from his bone and flesh, God makes the woman.

There is an order to all of creation: The Triunity (Father, Son, Holy Spirit); The Master Plan for All Creation; The Different Ranking Angels; The Heavens; Earth; Sun Moon; Stars; Water; Land; Plants; Ocean animals; Man; Land Animals; Woman; Generations; A Chosen People; Jesus; The Holy Spirit; The Church; Restoration; Dominion - The Kingdom.

So, we have the Great I AM, the Sovereign, The Almighty, Creator of all, whose story and origin, He will disclose, when, where, how, to whom, only when appropriate and when he deems convenient.

We have The Master Plan. Everything; above, below, yesterday, today, tomorrow, every contingency, every question, every answer, our DNA, the number of years of our existence, every one of our hairs numbered, Man's History from beginning to end, the many who will be called and the few that will be chosen, every single prophecy, every single covenant, leaders, lovers, traitors, every scenario and how it plays out; on and on, ad-infinitum.

Next, we have the Angels. [*Psalms 103:20 "Bless the LORD, ye his angels that excel in strength, that do his commandments, hearkening unto the voice of his word."*] Angels, Archangels, Seraphim and Cherubim. These marvelous beings, serve the Triunity. By our standards, they serve day and night; by His standards, eternally. They protect the Glory of God.

They are God's Generals. They are defenders of nations. They are beings of light. They travel with lightning speed to execute God's orders. They obey God's orders implicitly and explicitly. They minister to us, as directed by God. They bring us His revealed word, according to the Master Plan. They act as our defenders on a spiritual level. They protect and escort us, through the valley of shadow of death. They can take on human form and in so doing, are capable of performing human roles. They, existed way before the creation of the earth.

The rest of the order: The Heavens; Earth; Sun Moon; Stars; Water; Land; Plants; Ocean Animals; Man; Land Animals; Woman; Generations; A Chosen People; Jesus; The Holy Spirit; The Church; Restoration; Dominion - The Kingdom; follows the prescribed program, as outlined by God, in the Bible.

In the sequence of events, once the man and the woman are created, the command to [*"Be fruitful, and multiply, and replenish the earth, and subdue it: and have dominion over the fish of the sea, and over the fowl of the air, and over every living thing that moveth upon the earth." Genesis 1:28*], was given by God.

In Chapter 15 of this book, we read about how Satan was instrumental, in living up to his definition of adversary. We learned of his cunning way of dealing with human life, in order to get mankind to renounce the God of Creation. As such, in the beginning, his strategy for the corruption of mankind goes into effect. Since there were only two humans in the world, he couldn't very well use human form to influence the Lords of this new creation. He had no grip, no handle on the situation. He had to act fast. This was the first family unit. If he could some way affect them, before the birth of their first child, the rest of humanity would be contaminated and then he would be worshipped, for giving humans the ability of knowing good and evil as God knew it.

The question still remained. How do you get to something pure, innocent, without sin, if there was never before, an exposure to this type of manipulation?

The key to opening a locked door from the inside, is to knock from the outside. It is up to the person inside, whether or not, to open the door. In today's society, we have security systems and at least a "peep hole", to assess if whomever is outside the door, is worthy of being received at the door or allowed to come inside. The person on the inside controls the door. She/he is looking to see if the one knocking, is a friend, someone of authority, or some other credible source. Well…leave it to the deceiver, the adversary, to figure it out, and he did. His solution would not only impact humanity, but as a bonus, would impact the animal kingdom as well.

Adam was made by God directly. The woman was made by God but from the man. To a certain degree, one might say that Adam's faith was stronger by being created first, having direct training and imprinting, of the Divine nature of God. Eve, on the other hand, had Adam primarily, as a physical reference point to humanity, and God as a "secondary" all together divine spiritual being. This is not to say that she was weaker. Just pointing out, that she would have been less prepared, until Adam would spend more time with her. As his help meet, Eve would have relied on Adam as Lord of this new creation, for her training and orientation.

[*Genesis 3:1 "Now the serpent was more subtil than any beast of the field which the LORD God had made. And he said unto the woman, Yea, hath God said, ye shall not eat of every tree of the garden?"*] The serpent was more 'subtil' or more subtle, meaning clever, than any of the beasts of the field which the Lord God had made.

Many questions, surround this passage of Scripture. Who or what was this serpent, which was wiser than the other animals? Why does the Bible employ the personal pronoun "he", instead of "it"? What do we know about the serpent in Genesis? He, apparently was able to speak, was non-threatening, was able to hear, was the male of the species, moved apparently erect throughout the garden and must have been quite a common sight, in the garden. Eve was not startled by its appearance, or surprised by any of its behavior. Why did the serpent choose Eve, instead of Adam for its conversation?

The serpent is used in Scripture, to represent Satan (in the Hebrew language), meaning an Adversary. He is the arch enemy of Jesus, believers, and humanity. As we learned before, from the book of Job, he is able to take on angelic form and seems indistinguishable, from the other angels. The one who can always identify him by nature, character and any form he takes, is God. His power is limited by God and at times is an instrument of God's righteousness. He lives up to his reputation as a liar, deceiver, tempter, murderer, thief and father of lies. In the Greek translation of the Bible he is known as diabolos or devil. Because he is the adversary, he is against anything that has to do with God or God's plans. He is an angelic being with rank. He has a series of spiritual beings that follow him and help him do his dirty work, these are known as 'daemon' or demons. Demons, are also enemies of God. They are believed to be angels who rebelled against God.

This is what the Bible says about Satan, the devil and demons:

> [Matthew 8:16 "When the even was come, they brought unto him many that were possessed with devils: and he cast out the spirits with his word…"]

> [Matthew 10:1 "And when he had called unto him his twelve disciples, he gave them power against unclean spirits, to cast them out…"]

> [Matthew 12:43-45 "When the unclean spirit is gone out of a man, he walketh through dry places, seeking rest, and findeth none. Then he saith, I will return into my house from whence I came out; and when he is come, he findeth it empty, swept, and garnished. Then goeth he, and taketh with himself seven other spirits more wicked than himself, and they enter in and dwell there: and the last state of that man is worse than the first. Even so shall it be also unto this wicked generation."]

> [James 2:19 "Thou believest that there is one God; thou doest well: the devils also believe, and tremble."]

[*Revelation 16:14* "For they are the spirits of devils, working miracles, which go forth unto the kings of the earth and of the whole world, to gather them to the battle of that great day of God Almighty."]

[*Luke 4:41* "And devils also came out of many, crying out, and saying, Thou art Christ the Son of God. And he rebuking them suffered them not to speak: for they knew that he was Christ."]

[*Matthew 25:41* "Then shall he say also unto them on the left hand, Depart from me, ye cursed, into everlasting fire, prepared for the devil and his angels:"]

[*Revelation 12: 7-9* "And there was war in heaven: Michael and his angels fought against the dragon; and the dragon fought and his angels, and prevailed not; neither was their place found any more in heaven. And the great dragon was cast out, that old serpent, called the Devil, and Satan, which deceiveth the whole world: he was cast out into the earth, and his angels were cast out with him"]

[*Ephesians 6:12* "For we wrestle not against flesh and blood, but against principalities, against powers, against the rulers of the darkness of this world, against spiritual wickedness in high places."]

Based on this information, I believe that the serpent speaking with Eve, is the devil taking on the only form he could in the beginning, in order to tempt Eve, to disobey God and introduce sin (disobedience) into humanity.

The serpent engages the woman in conversation. We

should not be shocked that the serpent speaks. Before making the woman, God creates the animals and brings them before Adam to be named. This tells us that the animals in the beginning, were able to understand human language, such as it was back then. Their capacity to understand may have been limited but communication they had. If we step forward into the time of Noah, before the flood, he called out to the animals and they came. It is very interesting to note in that story, that the animals came as described by God; in twos and representing each one of the species of their kind. They were not fighting over who would go first, second or last. They heard the voice of God through Noah and came to the prescribed location, on time, got into the Ark, into their assigned space and behaved accordingly, getting along with each other, for the journey of preservation and deliverance. Noah did not get the same response from the humans of his time. Somewhere in here, there is a lesson for us humans.

NOT JUST ANY TREE – NOT JUST ANY FRUIT

As far as the serpent, with all its attributes, it may have been the only animal with reasoning, capable of establishing dialogue and perhaps with its wisdom, it had gullibility. It had to be present whenever God was speaking to Adam in the garden. Its questions, were quite the opposite of what was originally said. One might say, that the interactive dialogue between Eve and the serpent, was contrary or adversarial. Let's consider the conversation between the serpent and Eve.

Serpent-

Genesis 3:1 "…hath God said, ye shall not eat of every tree of the garden?"] In other words, *"did God say that you should not eat of every tree in the garden?"* Notice the subtlety of specifying *"not eat of every tree."* This is not what God had said! The serpent was rephrasing God's words. The truth was being stretched just enough, for Eve to draw her own conclusion.

The serpent saw an opportunity to strike, at the newest member of creation. Eve, did not come "directly" from

God. She came from the same bone and flesh of Adam. She may not have had the strong spiritual relationship, which had been developed between God and Adam.

Having come from Adam, Eve had no other human counterpart with whom to compare or share information. She and Adam were it! Her direct relationship, would have been with Adam, as Adam's relationship was strong with God. Having come from Adam, as bone of his bone and flesh of his flesh, Eve would have looked up to Adam for instruction, direction, interpretation of the human feelings and emotions, that she encountered in her development.

In understanding her purpose, destiny and legacy, she would have aimed at helping Adam fulfill his purpose, destiny and legacy. Hearing about this tree of knowledge of good and evil, may have seemed as a good way to become better at helping Adam.

The purpose of her existence, would definitely play the biggest role in this creation. Eve was inquisitive in learning and understanding her role and position with regards to humanity. No alarms were sounding in her heart of pure innocence. She responds to the serpent's question.

Eve –

[*Genesis 3:2, 3 "We may eat of the fruit of the trees of the garden: But of the fruit of the tree which is in the midst of the garden, God hath said, Ye shall not eat of it, neither shall ye touch it, lest ye die."*] Eve starts out on the right path: *"we may eat of the fruit of the trees of the garden."* On the second part of her answer, she seems to forget an important detail. **Note**: *"…of the fruit of the tree which is in the midst of the garden…"* Her statement here, seems to indicate that there was only one tree, instead of two or that already in her mind, this particular tree, intrigued her. She may have been observing it or coming up to it frequently.

There were (2), two trees in the midst of the garden. [*Genesis 2:9 "…the tree of life also in the midst of the garden, and the tree of knowledge of good and evil."*] There was the tree of life and the tree of knowledge of good and evil. Her third phrase, seems to indicate she was absorbed in curiosity about what God had said and Adam taught her, regarding the tree. Her words to the serpent: *"…neither shall ye touch it, lest ye die."* God never said she could not touch it. He said: [*Genesis 2:17 "But of the tree of the knowledge of good and evil, thou shalt not eat of it: for in the day that thou eatest thereof thou shalt surely die."*] God specified the tree. He said: of the tree of the knowledge of good and evil, you shall not eat of it. He never said anything about touching it. It would seem that she considered, that there would be nothing wrong with touching the tree. Maybe, even the concept of death, had not yet been forged in her mind.

For being the most prudent animal in the garden, the serpent wasn't much on helping Eve's cause. It never offered a correction to her statement and just went with the flow.

Serpent

[*Genesis 3:4, 5 "…Ye shall not surely die: God doth know that in the day ye eat thereof, then your eyes shall be opened, and ye shall be as gods, knowing good and evil."*] Seems that the serpent had a piece of information that Eve was unaware of. *"You are not really going to die!"* is what the serpent was saying. At this point in time in her life, Eve may have not been witness to death. What may have been real in her mind, was that the tree of life, was right next to the tree of knowledge of good and evil, if death were to come, she could reach out to the tree of life, eat that fruit and not die. Of course we, were not there. All we have is what has been written.

The serpent continues: *"God doth know that in the day ye eat thereof..."* as if to say "God is aware that you will eat of this tree one day." When that happens. On that particular day *"your eyes shall be opened, and ye shall be as gods, knowing good and evil."*

By saying that *"her eyes would be opened"* the serpent was not implying that her eyes were closed, but that her understanding would open up to a new kind of knowledge. She and Adam would be at the same level of comprehension in good and evil, as the Triunity. From this point forward, we don't hear anymore about the crafty serpent.

DESIRE/LUST – KEY TO UNLOCKING KNOWLEDGE OF GOOD AND EVIL

This is what the Bible says in verse 6: *"And when the woman saw that the tree was good for food, and that it was pleasant to the eyes, and a tree to be desired to make one wise, she took of the fruit thereof, and did eat, and gave also unto her husband with her; and he did eat."* Before we discuss this verse, we need to go back to Chapter 2 and verse 9, where it reads as follows: *"out of the ground made the LORD God to grow every tree that is pleasant to the sight, and good for food"*. The key phrase that we want to look at in verse 9 is *"every tree that is pleasant to the sight, and good for food"*. When or what day, the woman finds herself admiring this tree, is not specified in the Bible.

Notice that the woman sees exactly what God wanted her to see: *"the woman saw that the tree was good for food, and that it was pleasant to the eyes."* Her obedience to God, was still intact up to this point. However, as we read further, notice the next phrase: *"a tree to be desired to make one wise."*

> [Jeremiah 17:9 "The heart is deceitful above all things, and desperately wicked…"]

> [James 1:14, 15 *"But every man is tempted, when he is drawn away of his own lust, and enticed. Then when lust hath conceived, it bringeth forth sin: and sin, when it is finished, bringeth forth death."*]

The woman seems to have stopped looking with the factual information of the knowledge received from God and Adam, and begins to process in her own mind *"a tree to be desired to make one wise."* From Eve's conversation with the serpent, a thought was planted into her mind. She takes the truth of what God said, with a little but deliberate deviation implanted by the serpent and comes up with her own conclusion *"the knowledge that I desire and the wisdom I need."* Temptation therefore, comes from within. It takes a conscious effort, a lust, and a desire, in order to sin.

The stimulus may be outside of the body, but it is the person, who deliberately sins from the inside. The devil or Satan does not make you sin. You do! Satan is an agent of deceit, among other terms, that we have already presented.

Notice: repentance is not for the devil or Satan. It is for humans who need to bring back their minds, from their selfish mental desires. Humans that have been enslaved, to think they are right or justified, in indulging or doing what they think is right. Without thinking, or facing the consequences of the lifestyle they are living, mankind faces the same justice as Satan. [*Matthew 25:41 "Then shall he say also unto them on the left hand, Depart from me, ye cursed, into everlasting fire, prepared for the devil and his angels…"*]

My dear reader, don't jump to conclusions just yet. We have a few more things to consider.

A few questions came into my head and perhaps you may have a few of your own. Where was God during this serpent/Eve conversation? Where was Adam? Why did God permit this to go on, right in front of Himself?

> The stimulus may be outside of the body, but it is the person, who deliberately sins from the inside. The devil or Satan does not make you sin. You do!

As I pondered these questions, the Holy Spirit provided some insight. As to the question of where was God? God was there! He was obviously observing, how the first human couple, were going to deal with this situation. This planet was going to be their dominion. They needed to start taking responsibility for what was given to them. God already had a plan of redemption built in to his Master Plan for whatever decisions mankind would take.

As to where was Adam? Adam was there with Eve. We read in [*Genesis 3:6 "...she took of the fruit thereof, and did eat, and gave also unto her husband with her..."*] Adam was there during the dialogue and when Eve took the fruit, ate from it and gave to him, he also ate of the fruit.

I imagine that Adam was also intrigued by the fruit of the tree of knowledge of good and evil. He was listening to the conversation between the serpent and Eve. In his mind, he may have been questioning what God had said about death, in relation to this tree. Adam offers no resistance or argument to Eve, as she shares the fruit with him. Eve did not seduce him. The desire of his heart, is what led him to eat of the fruit. Once again, God's sovereignty allowed this happen, as mankind needed to make decisions on their own.

Within that sovereignty, and as Father to Adam and Eve as the Triunity's children and first family, God needed to step in and deal with disobedience or sin. Then and there, He set boundaries. God needed to set a precedence in this new creation. The infection of sin to humankind, needed to be judged before it escalated to the rest of humanity, not yet born.

[*Genesis 3:7 "the eyes of them both were opened, and they knew that they were naked; and they sewed fig leaves together, and made themselves aprons."*] The effects of the fruit were apparently instantaneous. They looked at each other and realized they were naked. In other words, they saw themselves nude and were ashamed of each other "privately and personally." They sewed fig leaves together and made themselves aprons. Transparency was defeated! The great cover-up begins: a metaphorical representation of lies, an apron of fig leaves.

If you stop to think about it, this was a temporary fix to which man did not give much importance. It was quick and painless. Let's make an apron out of fig leaves. They did not think that the leaves would wither, dry up and eventually would have to be replaced. Their nudity would once again come back the following day. Yet, another effect of the fruit from the tree temporary solutions to a long term problem.

Man and woman, husband and wife from the beginning were transparent with God and themselves. Nudity was part of their transparency. There was no shame. There was no guilt.

All it took was lust: a personal desire to go beyond the commandment of God. All it took, was one person; albeit an important person, to be encouraged in the desire of the heart by an outside source.

Transparency between God, man, woman and nature had been severed. Man would no longer see eye to eye with God or with fellow man. The chain of events of a raging knowledge, without the wisdom and guidance from God, released what the serpent expected to happen. The open eyes: the awareness of new concepts, ideas, travesties, snares, traps, plots against one another by mankind, hate, rage and a host of innumerable emotions and desires, that from now, would become a part of mankind. A kind of "Pandora's box" had been opened.

[*Genesis 3:8 "And they heard the voice of the LORD God walking in the garden in the cool of the day: and Adam and his wife hid themselves from the presence of the LORD God amongst the trees of the garden."*] Having eaten of the tree, Adam and his wife are walking in the garden, in the cool of the day, possibly in the late afternoon. God had come to meet with them; perhaps in an accustomed place in the garden, to recap the events of the day. Not finding them there, God calls out to Adam: *"where are you?"*

The guilt of disobedience and the fear of death, was so great upon them, that they dreaded looking at the face of God. They hid themselves among the trees.

Here in lays a consequence of disobedience: Fear. Another: Hiding from the face of God. The problem: you can't hide from a God that can see everything.

Did God know where they were? Yes! Did he know why they were hiding? Yes! Why does God ask the question where are you, if he already knew their condition and their location? I believe that because God had a very close relationship with his children, He wanted them to respond in truth, about their present situation and condition. He also called out to Adam, because he was the one in charge, as head of the house and Lord of the new Creation.

Adam replies. [*Genesis 3:10 "I heard thy voice in the garden, and I was afraid, because I was naked; and I hid myself."*] Adam says "when you were calling me, I was afraid because I was naked and I hid myself". There was no "we" (as in my wife and I), in his statement. Out of fear of retaliation, he only thought about himself.

The effects of the fruit, were growing roots and branches, within the mindset of humanity. Fear, hiding, self-awareness, and shame.

[*Genesis 3:11 "And he said, who told thee that thou wast naked? Hast thou eaten of the tree, whereof I commanded thee that thou shouldest not eat?"*] In other words, God asks "how did you come about this knowledge that you are naked? Have you eaten from the tree I told you not to eat from? Have you disobeyed my commandment?"

[*Genesis 3:12 "The woman whom thou gavest to be with me, she gave me of the tree, and I did eat."*] Adam responds to God. It was the woman that you gave me. She gave me from the fruit of the tree and I ate it.

The fruit from the tree of knowledge of good and evil, continues to affect human thinking. He defers the consequence of his condition, to the wife. Disobedience does not accept blame. It is always someone else's fault. Mankind does not want to take ownership of disobedience or sin. It carries the penalty of death.

Once again, the effects of the fruit: short term thinking. He, does not realize that indirectly, his words are confessing, that it is God's fault because of the wife He gave him. Almost as if to say, "I would not have sinned, if you had not given me the woman".

Once sin nature takes over, you lose transparency out of fear. Clarity of thought is lost. You don't see the long term consequence of your actions. You sew an apron of fig leaves and put it on. You forget that by the next day your leaves have withered and died. You need to cover up again. You need, a longer lasting solution!

> Once sin nature takes over, you lose transparency out of fear. Clarity of thought is lost. You don't see the long term consequence of your actions.

[*Genesis 3:13 "The LORD God said unto the woman, what is this that thou hast done? And the woman said, the serpent beguiled me, and I did eat."*] God now confronts the woman. *"What have you done? Explain yourself."* Eve was a quick study.

Having heard Adam's accusation of her, she defends her part of the disobedience to the serpent. She says: *"the serpent seduced/tricked me and that is why I ate of the fruit."*

Yet another effect of the fruit shows up: Now there is accusation and complicity.

The exponential ramifications of mankind's end, from having disobeyed God's commandment, are seen by the Triunity. God's plan of redemption within the Master Plan, goes into effect by default, due to the human act of disobedience. It all ends up in the Divine Court Room, where the fate of this new creation, in its infancy, gets to be judged by a righteous Triune God.

HUMANITY'S AND SATAN'S TRIAL BEGINS

[*Genesis 3:14, 15 "And the LORD God said unto the serpent, because thou hast done this, thou art cursed above all cattle, and above every beast of the field; upon thy belly shalt thou go, and dust shalt thou eat all the days of thy life: and I will put enmity between thee and the woman, and between thy seed and her seed; it shall bruise thy head, and thou shalt bruise his heel."*] God as the Triunity, now addresses the serpent as the willing vessel of Satan and to Satan as having used the serpent, as its instrument of deception: *"because thou hast done this…"* In other words, because you have of your own mind, crafted, designed, devised this strategy, *"thou art cursed"* - you are cursed. Any privileges, form, or abilities you had before, are revoked. Your curse is *"above all cattle, and above every beast of the field"* - greater than that of domesticated or wild animals. *"Upon thy belly shalt thou go."* You will be moving about on your belly. *"Dust shalt thou eat all the days of thy life."* Because it would be moving upon its belly, the serpent's destiny would be, where the dust of the ground would forever be in its face and in its mouth. It may also have been a reminder to the serpent that since he decided to intervene with mankind, who was made from the dust, humanity would always be in its face and in its taste buds, for generations to come.

[Genesis 3:15 *"And I will put enmity between thee and the woman, and between thy seed and her seed; it shall bruise thy head, and thou shalt bruise his heel."*] God was direct. I will put hostility between you as the serpent and the woman. This hostility will be generational between your seed and her seed.

You may say to yourself, "Wait a minute, the woman does not carry the seed. The man carries the seed. She accepts the seed from man, nurtures it and gives it back to him as life." This is true. But in the woman, there was another seed. A seed that went back to before Adam. It was the seed of redemption. It was placed there by the Triunity, to be used when mankind would not be able to redeem itself. It was a "failsafe". That is why our God is so great. He took every contingency into consideration and pre-planned for it in his Master Plan.

At the beginning of our story, I spoke to you about how Adam received spiritual DNA. I spoke to you about how Adam's physical DNA had the "XX" gene. I explained how, when Adam was put to sleep, God took from the bone marrow of his rib, in order to make him his help meet. I also explained how the woman came to have the "XX" gene showing up in her present DNA and how man now has the "XY" gene. Man didn't lose a rib, he lost one part of the "XX" gene, in order to fulfill his destiny of multiplying and enriching the earth with mankind. The seed from Adam, in conjunction with Eve; bone of his bone and flesh of his flesh, would produce the offspring to populate the planet.

[Genesis 2:7 "...*man became a living soul.*"] By means of God breathing into the created man, a spiritual DNA was transferred into his physical being. He received two kinds of seed, a physical one which activated his flesh and bone and a Spiritual one, which activated his essence with the Triunity. The soul: the living essence of God himself, infused within the physical DNA of man, became Gods fingerprint of ownership. The failsafe for mankind.

God was telling the serpent, that the seed of the woman, would conquer the curse of death brought upon the soul of man, from eating of the tree of knowledge of good and evil. Sin nature was strategic to Satan's plan. That is why he attacks Eve. The sin that now was a part of her, would be a part of everyone else born from her.

The adversary sought to have won the adoration of humanity, by introducing them to an unbridled knowledge, which would put mankind on the same path of destruction he was on. God had foreseen his strategy. God had prepared for it. The collective Triunity had come into agreement, that when the adversary was to strike, a spiritual seed, one that would not have been stained by disobedience, would appear through the womb of the woman, to save humanity. The Son of God, Christ Jesus, born of God, without contamination from the seed of the serpent, would lead humanity back to its right path and be reconciled with God the Father.

The seed of the woman would break the thread of evil, Satan held over humanity's will. His example, his teachings, the faith and hope he would bring would break the curse of death. You, the serpent; the seed you have sown, will continue to bite humanity's heel. As you continue, generation after generation to attack man's heel (as in Achilles heel), to try and bring man down with your poison, your lies, deception, accusations, twisting of the truth, sowing doubt in the seed of Adam, eventually the seed of the woman will crush your head.

It was a warning! You messed with the innocence of my creation in its head. Eventually those innocent, will come to know the Truth and the Truth shall set them free. That truth, will step on your foundation of misused good and evil and will destroy the very head where it came from.

[*Genesis 3:16 "Unto the woman he said, I will greatly multiply thy sorrow and thy conception; in sorrow thou shalt bring forth children; and thy desire shall be to thy husband, and he shall rule over thee."*] God says to the woman, the pain of birth will be very strong. Whenever you have a child, you will know pain. My interpretation of what God has said is; "in the garden, your desire for knowledge, drove you to eat of the forbidden fruit. That act of disobedience, will bring pain to humanity. The pain you will feel, will be a constant reminder of your disobedience. I, should have been the object of your desire. However, your biggest desire from now on, will be to your husband. You will subject yourself to him. He will be your lord. He will govern you. He will rule over you. Good or bad, you will desire that man. You will be subjected to him". From that day forward, the woman would not be recognized as equal, because man became lord over her life. Notice that Sarah, Abraham's wife, after Eve, recalls the words of the God. [*Genesis 18:12 "Therefore Sarah laughed within herself, saying, after I am waxed old shall I have pleasure, **my lord** being old also"*]

[*Genesis 3:17 "And unto Adam he said… cursed is the ground for thy sake; in sorrow shalt thou eat of it all the days of thy life"*] My interpretation: God says to Adam Instead of listening to me and being obedient, you listened to the voice of your wife. Here is what will happen. The ground, is not going to be as good to you as it was before. In the beginning, it was nice and easy to tend to it. From now on, the soil will be tough, dry, will have rocks and stones, trees, stumps and all manner of debris. These will have to be cleaned before you plant it. It will grow weeds of all kinds, which will encroach on your soil. You are going to have to work very hard, in order for the earth to produce its food for you. You will be working on this earth, for the rest of your life.

[*Genesis 3:18 "Thorns also and thistles shall it bring forth to thee; and thou shalt eat the herb of the field."*] I believe this to say: the ground will produce grasses and plants, which will have thorns and rough edges that will hurt you as you grow your food. As a matter of fact, you will also learn to eat and use herbs and grasses that will grow in your field, for the confection of your food.

[*Genesis 3:19 "In the sweat of thy face shalt thou eat bread, till thou return unto the ground; for out of it wast thou taken: for dust thou art, and unto dust shalt thou return."*] I interpret this to mean:

as you work each day to clear the land, as you take out the weeds and protect the plants that you grow for food, from sun up to sun down, you are going to sweat. This is the cost of your disobedience. In order to eat, you will have to work and sweat. You will continue this cycle until you die. As a reminder, you came from dust and you will return to dust.

[*Genesis 3:21 "Unto Adam also and to his wife did the LORD God make coats of skins, and clothed them."*] Even in the course of disciplining Adam and Eve, God's mercy is shown. He knew, that the aprons of fig leaves, were not the appropriate covering for the shame that had come and would prevail in their lives, and the lives of the generations to come. It may have been God's way of showing them, that this experience would cost lives. Innocent lives would be sacrificed. This would be the reason for this passage. God would have had to kill an innocent animal, in order to provide a better covering for their shame: coats of skins. This would speak prophetically to the seed of the woman. The sacrificial lamb, who would take the sin of humanity away. The lamb that would be slain, in order to cover us with his blood, as redemption for our sin and provide a mantle of mercy, before the eyes of God.

> [*Genesis 3:22-24 "And the LORD God said, Behold, the man is become as one of us, to know good and evil: and now, lest he put forth his hand, and take also of the tree of life, and eat, and live forever. Therefore the LORD God sent him forth from the Garden of Eden, to till the ground from whence he was taken. So he drove out the man; and he placed at the east of the garden of Eden Cherubims, and a flaming sword which turned every way, to keep the way of the tree of life."*]

It is sad to read, how the first family was not strong enough to stand up to temptation. The very fountain of knowledge: their Creator, was ever present to provide for all their needs, wants, questions and development. The Triunity respected its creation. God knew that it was good. He loved his family. He wanted his family to grow and multiply under his care. He wanted to see them flourish as the trees and plants in his garden. Most of all, I believe He wanted his creation to love him back. That love, had to be earned, given, shared, demonstrated and respected. As perfect love was integral to the Triunity, so it should come, from this new creation. It could not be demanded, it had to grow and develop. What a lesson for humanity: Triunity sharing its deepest love. How humbling of Triunity.

In this beginning, God declares that the man had become as one of the Triunity, knowing good and evil. Corrupt as man was, a plan of redemption was put into effect by the Triunity. The tree of life was protected. Had Adam eaten, from the tree of life in his corrupted state, man would have never been able to obtain the opportunity of redemption. Going back into the Garden of Eden and eating of the tree of life, sin nature would have caused humanity its life. We, may never have been a part of this story.

The Garden of Eden, was like the first tabernacle. It was the open church or synagogue. No walls. Just God and man, having fellowship in His dwelling place. How delightful.

God's master Plan is still unfurling. He drove out the first family from the garden, so that the sanctuary would not be defiled. He placed Cherubims and a flaming sword, to block the way to the tree of life. He never gave up on the first family then and He is still overseeing their children now. We are the generation that will make a difference.

The story of humanity, with all its contrasts and manifestation from the fruit of the tree of knowledge of good and evil, and the serpent prince that now has dominion over them, is written in the Bible. God does not cover our dark past or bloody history. He gives it to us raw. In black and white upon the pages of the books of truth: The Bible. That Book, the Bible, is the Master Plan for humanity. It is being fulfilled by the Triunity.

Mankind, the planet, heaven and earth as we know it, will be restored. It will be the paradise it was meant to be. The makeover is coming. God is choosing unto himself a people, he will turn into a kingdom of priests.

> [*Exodus 19:6 "And ye shall be unto me a kingdom of priests, and a holy nation."*]

> [*1 Peter 2:9, 10 "But ye are a chosen generation, a royal priesthood, an holy nation, a peculiar people; that ye should shew forth the praises of him who hath called you out of darkness into his marvelous light: which in time past were not a people, but are now the people of God: which had not obtained mercy, but now have obtained mercy."*]

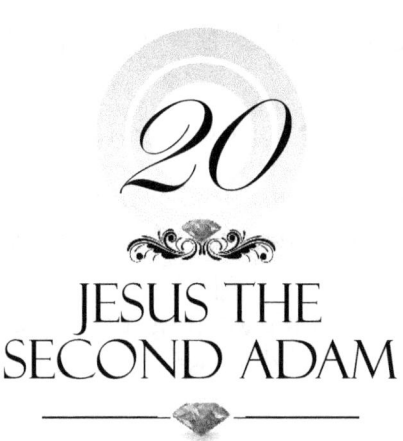

20
JESUS THE SECOND ADAM

The seed of the woman lay dormant for thousands of years. Mankind went from bad to worse. The fruit of the tree of knowledge of good and evil, was not only feeding mankind, it was engorging the serpent. All the characteristics that personified Satan, became prevalent in humanity. Lying, cheating, murder, deception, betrayal, hate, disobedience; brother against brother, sons against fathers and fathers against sons and love of self.

The light of true understanding: wisdom, science, knowledge, family, along with so many other good gifts from the Triunity, were now shrouded in darkness. Many prayed, having gone to the grave with the faith that a redeemer would come. Others, lost their faith and began to worship other gods.

Just a remnant, seemed to keep the faith of a Redeemer, alive. The timing had to be just right, for His advent.

From that remnant, prophets who kept their relationship with Triunity above the ever growing tide of humanity's dark side, became the voice of God (Elohim).

[*Isaiah 9:2 "The people that walked in darkness have seen a great light: they that dwell in the land of the shadow of death, upon them hath the light shined."*] People who had been walking in ignorance, whose mind or judgment was clouded; those who had been confused, those that were led astray, anyone with the presence of mind to see, hear, and learn the truth, would see a great light. They would finally see the truth of salvation, restoration and true justice.

Those condemned to death by the guilt of disobedience since Adam, would witness the light of deliverance shining upon them. Countless generations who died, who dwelled in the land of the shadow of death; the *"light of the world"* would cast away that shadow. In death, the light that was in Him would descend with him to that land with its shadow. He would bare testimony, that resurrection was not a myth.

[*Isaiah 9:6 "For unto us a child is born, unto us a son is given: and the government shall be upon his shoulder: and his name shall be called Wonderful, Counsellor, The mighty God, The everlasting Father, The Prince of Peace."*] For the Jewish people, the nation of Israel, a child would be born. Through the willing vessel of a woman called Mary, he would be born. For the rest of humanity, through divine intervention, a son would be given. He would be a male. He had to be the first born male, in order to receive all the benefits of a first born child. Yes, he would come from God's chosen people. He would come from the people of the covenant. He would be a child born from within that nation, that culture, that faith.

He would be much more than a child. He would be the Son of God. This would be Triunity's gift for salvation of mankind, as foreseen and implemented in the Master Plan. This *"son"* would make a difference. He would not follow in his human father's (Adam's) footsteps. He had to be conceived through divine intervention, so that the contamination that was being carried since Adam, could be cancelled out, inoculated, and neutralized.

[*Isaiah 7:15 "Butter and honey shall he eat, that he may know to refuse the evil, and choose the good."*] This meant that he would grow up just like other men. He would enjoy the food and be part of the community with its customs and rituals. He would not be treated any differently than anyone born in his time. His development, social skills, education, vocation and preparation for life, would not have special treatment. Only by being exposed to the reality of the world he was born in, would this child, this son, be able to refuse evil and choose all that is good.

The tree of knowledge of good and evil, whose nutritional value had influenced humanity incorrectly up until this time, would no longer spread distorted knowledge upon mankind, through this child; this son. Being human and yet divine (as Adam was), he would be subject to all temptations and failures of humanity. Being divine, he had the wisdom and knowledge, to make the correct decisions. The Son would show humanity, that it is possible to live in an earthen vessel and yet cultivate a spiritual life. An earthen vessel, would be worthy to the Father. His example would vindicate the Father's wrath for death. His humbleness, faith, love, mercy, compassion, righteousness, message, character and nature, would be a witness to his people and the rest of the world.

Just so that there would be no mistaking his identity, the prophecy spoke unerringly of his identification and the power that was given to Him. The *"government shall be upon his shoulder."* Law, justice, righteousness; the implementation of fair, equitable and truthful delivery, in matters of faith and law in the affairs of men, would be his burden of liability and responsibility. He would establish his Kingdom, he would establish his rule.

The names by which he would be recognized, determined the length and breadth of his authority:

Wonderful Full of wonders miracles acts which defy the laws of science or reason.

Counsellor One who gives orientation or guidance to others or one who listens to the concerns of others and delivers the best assessment on a course of action.

The *Mighty God* The God of Power Not abusive power but firm and benevolent power.

The *Everlasting Father* Meaning that as the Son, He would be the eternal embodiment of his Father. He would represent the everlasting relationship of Father and Son as being one.

The *Prince of Peace* To differentiate between his Father as the King and himself, as being the Prince.

The second Adam was a gift. He was given. [*John 3:16, 17*

"For God so loved the world that he gave his only begotten Son, that whosoever believeth in him should not perish, but have everlasting life. For God sent not his Son into the world to condemn the world; but that the world through him might be saved".]

BONE OF MY BONES and FLESH OF MY FLESH / 138

THE GIFT

You would have to be some kind of father, willing to believe in humanity's cause for redemption, that you would give up your only son, to be born in a corrupted world and have enough faith, that your son would not be persuaded, influenced and or seduced, so that through him, humanity would be saved. You would have to trust the family that would receive this gift, enough that they would provide the correct moral code, a strong faith base and a nurturing ambiance, for the purpose which was predestined in him, before coming into this world. Only one Father I know, would do this. The Father of Creation. He alone, who could foresee the future, chose the right couple, the right time and the right place in history, for the coming of His Son.

Without getting into too much detail about the city, the state, the country, political structure and economics of the time, which can be seen throughout history, let's consider briefly, the family that would receive the gift.

Mary was a teenage girl, who was never married before or

had not entered into any sexual relationship, with a man. She was engaged to be married. Through the customs of the time, it was a pre-arranged marriage. She and her husband to be, had not lived together. The Bible clearly states that she was a virgin. [Luke 1:26, 27 *"And in the sixth month the angel Gabriel was sent from God unto a city of Galilee, named Nazareth, to a virgin espoused to a man whose name was Joseph, of the house of David; and the virgin's name was Mary."* This pre-arranged marriage, was as binding as if she were legally married in today's society.

This would be Mary's first child. She was not an experienced mother. She may have done "baby sitting" in her time and would have been exposed to children, as our own children are exposed to brothers and sisters, cousins and other relatives. At any rate, early teen pregnancies in our western society, have become common place and accepted in the metropolitan culture.

In Mary's time, a teen pregnancy and one where a pre-arranged marriage was involved, would have made front page news and media outrage, to the point of stoning the poor girl to death.

This, was the woman God chose to be the bearer of His child, Jesus.

Mary's husband to be, was named Joseph. A general building contractor of his time, specializing in all aspects of carpentry. A humble, just and respectable man who was working in his own business and was making plans for his own family. He hailed from the lineage of King David.

Not much of a biography, for the man who was to become the stepfather of the Almighty's son.

Now imagine with me, as Mary came to grips with the news that she would be the mother of Jesus. How was she going to explain this to Joseph? It was great news!

However, how do you explain a supernatural phenomenon to a very natural man? How do you tell your husband that you are pregnant but it is not his child? How can you even begin to approach this? It is not like you can keep this quiet, when the evidence was sure to grow! What would Joseph do? What would the community, the religious leaders, friends and relatives say, when they hear about the Joseph and Mary scandal? How was this going to affect Joseph's business and business partners? What about his career?

In today' time, the news media would have a field day. F.B. statements would keep the internet pages on fire, for weeks. Stop to think of all those women who thought that they would be the chosen one. Tweeter this and tweeter that. The blogs would still be ranting to this day.

As you can see, the birth of Christ was a very controversial situation. The Bible does not give a very detailed account of what went on in the minds of Joseph and Mary, when the news by the Archangel Gabriel, settled in their hearts. Joseph was already planning on the divorce. Had it not been for the fact that Gabriel himself came to give Joseph an explanation, Jesus' stepfather may have had another name.

These were the chosen parents of Jesus. From the onset, we can see the family dynamics of culture, religion, politics and multitasking that was taking place not just in the natural but also in the supernatural. We can perceive the change taking place on earth as it is in heaven.

The pregnant Mary goes to visit her cousin Elisabeth and spends almost three months with her. Nothing like a seasoned woman of God, to mentor and coach you, for the coming of Christ. The presence of the Holy Spirit is so strong in Mary that when greeting Elisabeth from the door, just the sound of her voice, stirs the joy of baby John inside her and fills her with the Holy Spirit. (There is much to be said here about a Spiritual connection…but that is another story).

Adam and Eve were our perfect parents. God made them to provide for us in every way. As with Jesus, God would have been there from the beginning, to see us develop as His gifted children, in the government of His Kingdom.

Sin nature, beginning with Adam and Eve, denied us entry into the Kingdom. The birth of Eve's offspring came into life, from a mom and dad that were tainted by sin. The results are seen in the first homicide (Cain and Abel). Sin nature also gave us something in the beginning, which was more important than condemnation: the gift of God's mercy. Not only was it demonstrated in His treatment of discipline to our first parents but demonstrating it, as in the seed of the woman. A promise of redemption through grace, way back in time, comes in the form of the second Adam, known as Jesus, our Redeemer.

Mary was the bearer of that seed. She was chosen from the beginning. Where Eve's child Cain, kills Abel, due to the sin nature, Mary's righteous child Jesus, is also killed and brings hope faith and restoration. The death of Eve's righteous child, Abel, for offering up the sacrifice of a lamb to God for his sins, is now vindicated by the Lamb of God, killed by the unrighteous sons of Cain to redeem everyone who believes in Him. In truth, Abel became his brother's keeper.

> [Hebrews 11:4 "By faith Abel offered unto God a more excellent sacrifice than Cain, by which he obtained witness that he was righteous, God testifying of his gifts: and by it he being dead yet speaketh"]

> [Hebrews 12:24 "And to Jesus the mediator of the new covenant, and to the blood of sprinkling, that speaketh better things than that of Abel."]

Sin nature also gave us something in the beginning, which was more important than condemnation: the gift of God's mercy. Not only was it demonstrated in His treatment of discipline to our first parents but demonstrating it, as in the seed of the woman. A promise of redemption through grace, way back in time, comes in the form of the second Adam, known as Jesus, our Redeemer.

BONE OF MY BONES and FLESH OF MY FLESH / 144

22

THE FAMILY AND THE BIBLE

Jesus, Son of God, birthed by Mary and fathered by Joseph, presents us, with a less than perfect family. By reading Scripture, you can see that the life of Jesus, in prophecy and birth right, contains so many challenges that it would seem nearly impossible, for the child of God to survive and let alone be an example, of human success in a messed up society.

These are the things, which the inspired written Word of God presents, to a world that thinks that it cannot change and is just set for gloom and doom. We as a society, have allowed men and women, without the wisdom of God, to dictate what everyone in their own mind thinks, is best for us and this planet. The concern that I have, is not freedom of speech. My concern is, that the wisdom of men in today's society, has been based for so long on independent thinking, that the Father and giver of science, knowledge, and wisdom has been purposely kept away from his children. The expressed behavior is the same as adolescents, who seem to think that they know it all;

parents are "old school" and only their contemporaries, really know what is happening. Only they get it! Mom and dad don't!

Granted, there are some parents that because of their particular circumstances, may not have had the understanding to deal with a myriad of scenarios that affect their children. This is the reason, that fathers or mothers, are not necessarily the ones who give birth but the ones who undertake the responsibility for lovingly taking under their wings, those that lack a father or mother figure. God, has provided those who seek Him, a mentor, a counselor, a granddad or grandma, a stepfather, a friend; someone other than the biological father or mother, that will help shape the future outcome of that man or woman.

Family is dear to the Triunity. They could not function or present a model of family, if they themselves were not representatives of that lifestyle.

Jesus was not just planted in the ground like a seed, expected to sprout and then join a family. God saw to it in eternity, that he, would come into a loving family. Not a perfect family but one that would give him the skills and upbringing that would balance out his spiritual, as well as his physical character.

Joseph and Mary were not special. They couldn't be. Jesus needed to come into this world like any other child without special privileges. This was, so that no one could single him out for not complying with the law or the character traits of humanity. He needed to be natural in every way. It was the responsibility of the Father, to see to the wellbeing of His Son. In this, he would set an example for humanity.

Later on in life, when Jesus comes to the crucifixion, like His Father had taught by example, He also takes care of his earthly mother, Mary. He assigns her care to his best friend, the Apostle John. [*John 19: 25-27 "Now there stood by the cross of Jesus his mother, and his mother's sister, Mary the wife of Cleophas, and Mary Magdalene. When Jesus therefore saw his mother, and the disciple standing by, whom he loved, he saith unto his mother, Woman, behold thy son! Then saith he to the disciple, Behold thy mother! And from that hour that disciple took her unto his own home."*]

BONE OF MY BONES and FLESH OF MY FLESH / 148

THE BRIDE OF JESUS THE DIVINE

It was at the cross and post mortem, that Jesus gives birth to his bride. Just as Adam was not meant to be alone and God created for him a help meet (his bride), Jesus the Divine would not be left alone, without a help meet or his bride.

We often think, why did Jesus not marry? We speculate based on our own physical wants and desires, that Jesus could have had an affair. He could have had children and so on and so forth.

Our speculation is based on western thought and not on eastern culture, where the Bible was written. During the time of Christ, cultural and family traditions were much different than our views in western society. Marriages were pre-arranged by the families from early childhood, same as in some foreign cultures. The bride and groom did not have much say in the decision. There were properties, land, livestock, businesses and so much more that had to be considered and protected, which could not just fall into the hands of anyone family. Marriage was like the merger of two large corporations, a lot of consideration had to be given as to the present and future assets of the new enterprise.

Jesus was not just the Son of God, He was an ambassador, a Prince, the only begotten of the Father. His actions, character, nature and profile, all had to fall in line with who he was in the flesh as well as in the Heavenly Kingdom. His demeanor in the affairs of his Father, would have serious consequences in heaven and earth.

Due to his nature and character, his bride needed to have his same character and nature. There was a lot at stake here. His bride would have to live eternally. Her love would have to be personal and universal. She would have to embrace all of humanity. Give her love to everyone and yet be private and intimate with Jesus. She would have to respect the wishes of her father-in-law. She would have to be powerful in her own right. She must be able to wield the power of the Holy Spirit; must be able to speak all languages. She would represent every woman in God's Kingdom. She would need to understand every need and want of her husband and be the nurturing mother to all their children. No earthly woman could have filled those shoes.

As with Adam, whose wife came from him, so it would be with Jesus the Divine. Adam was put to sleep (a symbol of death and resurrection), an incision was made on his side, a rib was extracted and a help meet created, as bone of his bone and flesh of his flesh.

We see the parallel in Jesus. He was pronounced dead on the cross, the soldier pierced his side, blood and water came out of him (this process was symbolic in Adam but made reality in the life of Christ). This is the same process, as when a woman gives birth (blood and water). His death and resurrection gives him divine power to bring into being, his bride, which we know now as the church.

How do we know that the church is the bride of Christ? We need to take a closer look at the New Testament writing of Matthew. [*Matthew 16:15-18 "He saith unto them, But whom say ye that I am? And Simon Peter answered and said, Thou art the Christ, the Son of the living God. And Jesus answered and said unto him, Blessed art thou, Simon Barjona: for flesh and blood hath not revealed it unto thee, but my Father which is in heaven. And I say also unto thee, that thou art Peter, and upon this rock I will build my church; and the gates of hell shall not prevail against it."*]

Jesus had just arrived at the coasts of Caesarea Philippi. He is speaking with the disciples and he asks them a question: *"Whom do men say that I, the Son of man, am?"* The disciples all gave an answer. Jesus makes the question more specific, as it applied to them who had been with him for some time. His question: *"But whom say ye that I am?"* Only Peter's answer stood out. Peter says: *"Thou art the Christ, the Son of the living God."* Jesus blessed Peter because his answer was not one that came from the onslaught of public opinion. Peter's answer came, as a result of revelation from God himself. This is why Jesus says: *"for flesh and blood hath not revealed it unto thee, but my Father which is in heaven"*. The revelation, word of knowledge, which Peter received, came directly from God the Father. This statement was foundational, in the work that was to be undertaken by the disciples. This declaration by Peter, which did not come from human thought, would be the ever establishing foundation of the bride of Christ: the church. In other words, this confession, of Jesus as the Son of the Living God by a Jewish man, meant that the bride of Christ would embrace him as Messiah. Humanity was ready for its Redeemer.

In John Chapter 20, after his resurrection, Jesus does something that God did with Adam. In Genesis we read [*Genesis 2:7 "And the LORD God formed man of the dust of the ground, and breathed into his nostrils the breath of life; and man became a living soul."*] It states that God breathed into the first man's nostrils and he became a living soul.

As the man could not live without the breath of life from God, without His spiritual DNA, neither could the bride of Christ be born without his Spiritual DNA and the breath of life. In other words, the bride of Christ, which was about to be born, needed the Spirit of the one who was going to be her husband in order to be his help meet. [*John 20:22 "And when he had said this, he breathed on them, and saith unto them, Receive ye the Holy Ghost."*] This impartation of breath from Jesus, not only echoed the will of God for humanity, it fulfilled the promise of Genesis 3:15 regarding the seed of the woman.

The love of Jesus, as the Son of God, could not and would not be limited to the love of one woman on earth. His love, was the same love of His Father for all his children. This is why the church was born: to be the love of all humanity in one body, in one harmonious co-existence; the Creator and his creation united forever. Flesh and bone transcending beyond the natural to the supernatural. In Christ, God's children will have the peace and harmony to perpetuate the Master Plan, under the direction and guidance of the Triunity.

This is why in the book of Revelation, in the final chapter of the Master Plan, there is an open invitation to all believers:

> [*Revelation 22:17 "And the Spirit and the bride say, Come. And let him that hears say, Come. And let him that is athirst come. And whosoever will, let him take the water of life freely."*]

> [*John 3:29 "He that hath the bride is the bridegroom: but the friend of the bridegroom, which stands and hears him, rejoices greatly because of the bridegroom's voice: this my joy therefore is fulfilled."*]

> [*Revelation 21:9 "And there came unto me one of the seven angels which had the seven vials full of the seven last plagues, and talked with me, saying, Come hither, I will shew thee the bride, the Lamb's wife."*]

> [*Revelation 21:2 "And I John saw the holy city, new Jerusalem, coming down from God out of heaven, prepared as a bride adorned for her husband."*]

BONE OF MY BONES and FLESH OF MY FLESH

RESPONSIBILITIES OF THE WIFE AND THE HUSBAND

At the conclusion of the last chapter, we see a glorious event of the eventual wedding of Jesus Christ to his bride the Church. However, anyone that has been a wedding planner or through experience, has gone through this much anticipated and anxious ceremony, knows that it takes time and resources to accomplish this spectacular celebration. The list seems endless, and while the bride is still young, tutoring is through the Word.

This is why Bone of my Bone and Flesh of my Flesh has been God's assignment in my life. The bride needs to get ready. We the church, the bride of the Lamb, need to make final preparations. Only the Father knows the time and the place of the reception. The reception hall is prepared. The invitations have been sent. It is up to the guests to respond or not. This is a Royal wedding. All nations will be invited. Heavenly guests will be watching the fulfillment of a once in a lifetime event. The Bride needs to know her place and the requirements for this most auspicious event.

Companionship

Companionship was the reason from the beginning, for Adam's help meet. As Adam represented the beginning of Humanity, he could not do it alone. God himself stated that it was not good for man to be alone. The life that was drawn from Adam, was given to him in the form of Eve.

God the Father of the bride and the father of the groom, gives her away to the man. He officiates the ceremony. He makes the pronouncement. He gives them the mandate. He blesses them and releases them into the prepared garden he has set up for them.

From the beginning, they were a part of each other. He was incomplete without her and she was incomplete without him. There were animals, birds, fish and insects and now man had a companion. The responsibilities of maintaining the garden and looking after God's creation was much easier now. The mandate to be fruitful and multiply could now be carried on by the newlyweds. The two could now be one in companionship and intimacy.

Sin nature saw to it that this holy bond be broken and the knowledge received was corrupted. Through guesswork and immediate remediation, man has tried to patch things up. Humanity knows, that the knowledge of the Creator is required but He is avoided. It seems that every day a new group, a new way of thinking, a subtle approach to whitewash evil, is presented to our society. Anything that has the name of God or is associated with God, is slowly being erased. The more society pushes for this obliteration, the more it strips itself away from the shroud of morality and under the mantle of depravation. However, not everyone will succumb. There is a remnant. There will be a remnant. The olive tree is not dead. New branches are being grafted to it. The Holy Spirit is the fountain of living water that will make it happen.

Having lost the original compass bearing, God provides guidance and direction to the wife, the bride, the church, in order to be healed and ready for Christ.

> [*Ephesians 5:22-33 "Wives, submit yourselves unto your own husbands, as unto the Lord. For the husband is the head of the wife, even as Christ is the head of the church: and he is the savior of the body. Therefore as the church is subject unto Christ, so let the wives be to their own husbands in everything. Husbands, love your wives, even as Christ also loved the church, and gave himself for it; that he might sanctify and cleanse it with the washing of water by the word, that he might present it to himself a glorious church, not having spot, or wrinkle, or any such thing; but that it should be holy and without blemish. So ought men to love their wives as their own bodies. He that loves his wife loves himself. For no man ever yet hated his own flesh; but nourishes and cherishes it, even as the Lord the church: for we are members of his body, of his flesh, and of his bones. For this cause shall a man leave his father and mother, and shall be joined unto his wife, and they two shall be one flesh. This is a great mystery: but I speak concerning Christ and the church. Nevertheless, let every one of you in particular so love his wife even as himself; and the wife see that she reverence her husband."*]

In the current state of marriage, at least in the U.S.A. and more so in the Church, the undermining of the Word of God, as a valid source of educating and preparing the man and the woman for the responsible attainment of companionship, has led to the degradation of respect and honor in the roles of a divine order. The end result is, the lack of peace and understanding within the home. So, let's consider the reasoning behind the Scriptural wisdom, in order to stabilize the marriage and prepare the church as the Bride of the Lamb.

> Having lost the original compass bearing, God provides guidance and direction to the wife, the bride, the church, in order to be healed and ready for Christ.

"Wives, submit yourselves unto your own husbands, as unto the Lord." The word submit does not mean slavery. Because the term is used in the Word of God, and in our translation of the original, it does not mean that there is to be a contractual obligation of slavery, when a couple marries. It does mean, coming into agreement, after careful consideration by the husband and wife on the presumed conflict. Both husband and wife, after seeking the Lord in prayer, will sit at the table and rationally, faithfully and in love make a decision which is mutually agreeable. In this sense, one submits to the other. Yielding, allows for the free flow of traffic and also opens the lanes of communication.

Another meaning for this word is, abiding. From the root word abode, referring to the place where both live. Abide with me, means to live with me. It means to share my residence. The one making the offer, has control over the rules of abiding. The person to whom the offer is made, has the prerogative of accepting or not, once the conditions of abiding have been explained. The one accepting the offer to abide, must be in agreement with the rules of the abode. The person accepting the rules of the abode, is submitting or abiding. If there are conditions which have changed in the course of abiding, these must be discussed. It becomes a negotiation, where both parties amicably seek submission from each other, in order to continue abiding in harmony.

Why is this statement instituted in the word of God? It goes back to Genesis when the woman disobeys God's commandment of not eating from the tree of knowledge of good and evil. We discussed it in chapter 17, regarding the tree of knowledge of good and evil. [*Genesis 3:16 "Unto the woman he said, I will greatly multiply thy sorrow and thy conception; in sorrow thou shalt bring forth children; and **thy desire shall be to thy husband**, and he shall rule over thee."*] It was the woman's initial desire for the tree, which caused the disobedience. Now, her desire is redirected to her husband who would govern over her. As such, the church is now subject to the government by Christ. She must submit/abide in him, in order to part-take of the rewards offered by the husband.

"For the husband is the head of the wife, even as Christ is the head of the church: and he is the savior of the body". The explanation here is, that the husband becomes the overseer of the work

of the woman, as it relates to the home, in much the same way as Christ is the overseer in the work of the church. There is another caveat in the text, which has a saving grace. This not only applies to the church, it applies as well to the home. Christ is the savior of the body. The body is the church. The church is comprised of men and women, husbands and wives and extended families. As in the case of Christ being the savior of the body, so must the man be the savior and protector of the woman and his home. This is man's first church and ministry.

"Therefore as the church is subject unto Christ, so let the wives be to their own husbands in everything." As the bride (the church), is subject to the groom (Christ), the wives need to abide with their husbands in everything, not just some things. The need of the wife to abide, represents the order of the church. If the husband and wife are not in agreement in love, companionship, education, discipline, budgets, investments and so many other responsibilities of the family, how then the church, which is made up of the families or the body, will be able to present to the world, a well-structured loving family as Christ as its head? The mutual submission, recognizing the husband as the head of household, is a representation of the priesthood in the home; it points the way to Christ being the priest and head of the church.

"Husbands, love your wives, even as Christ also loved the church, and gave himself for it;" Here is wisdom for all men: If the wife is to subject herself in everything, as the church is subject to Christ, then the statement applies that the

husband must (this is not a conditional statement), love the wife to the point that as a man, you must be willing to give up your life for her.

In western society, we assume this responsibility, when we go before the civil authorities, procure the license to marry and celebrate after the public pronouncement. When the Bible was written, the pre-arranged marriage was in force, the moment the parents agreed on it. That is why Joseph, who was betrothed to Mary, considered a divorce. They had not consumed the obligations of their marriage but were legally bound to uphold them.

Looking at it from our culture, a lot of what goes on in the marriage and the lack of submission or support, is because we are not willing to abide. The pre-nuptial agreements are arranged by attorneys. It is not by the head of the families who have the best interest in mind of their son or daughter. Marriage in today's society, has become a test of trial and error. The problem with this scenario is, that no one wants to take responsibility for their actions or that someone ends up taking all responsibility. The other test member, continues the exploration, causing more pain than good, by satisfying selfish desires without responsible submission.

"That he might sanctify and cleanse it with the washing of water by the word," This is the action of a loving Christ with his church. He gave himself for it: to sanctify and cleanse it with the washing of water by the word. Christ wants to make the church holy. The fact that it requires sanctification, means that there are sacrifices. If there is

cleansing, that means that there must be dirty laundry or circumstances that have prevailed, requiring the cleansing. There is a washing by water that needs to take place. It is the baptism. The symbol of burying what is dead and coming to new life. There is a washing that needs to take place by the word: counseling, advice, positive communication and admonition without accusation.

"That he might present it to himself a glorious church, not having spot, or wrinkle, or any such thing; but that it should be holy and without blemish." Once again, Christ sets the standard in the marriage relationship of husband and wife. Why the sacrifice, the sanctification, the cleansing, the washing, the word? Because the wife, like the church, is a representation of the husband. She is the one that gives credibility, honor, and respect, to the work and character of her husband.

A dark spot in a white gown can be noticed from quite a distance. It represents those little things that we often try to hide but that are very visible. It is human nature to try and conceal facts and past actions that will eventually show up. These things have to be addressed. Transparency, integrity and honesty are keys to preserving the marriage. God wants the bride to be spotless for his Son.

Wrinkles, are the obvious faults. They show up as unwanted lines and creases in our clothing. It speaks of habits that we need to iron out. Often times, to remove a wrinkle, you need to spray or sprinkle some water on it and apply a warm iron to the surface. You just can't apply the hot iron to any cloth. Each cloth has its own properties. You have to move the iron in the right direction in order to smooth out the wrinkle. Permanent wrinkles are those that you try to iron out and they tend to always come back. They represent faults or flaws in character that only God can remove. It means that the fibers in the cloth are so damaged that the only way to fix them, is to replace the garment. As the bride/wife of the Lord, only the Holy Spirit, His word and obedience, will help us remove the wrinkles in the marriage relationship. We, as the Body of Christ can't have wrinkles or any such things.

Holy and without blemish speaks of two things. The first thing is holiness. It means being separated for the designed purpose to which you are called. It means that you are consecrated to the service of God. There is a process of purification; call it training or education by which you acquire luster and polish, to be in the presence of the royal court. It is the Proverbs 31 woman, the Esther and the Priesthood of the temple.

The second thing, the blemish, refers to dings, dents, aberrations in the form of character. It is like going to the store to buy a silver cup. You inspect it and find that it does not meet your expectation of relative perfection. As you hold it up to the light, it is tarnished in some areas. It has dents in its form. There are rough surfaces. The way it was polished shows lack of care and appreciation of its value. Blemishes are things that affect the beauty and value of an object. Because blemishes are your character traits, you may want to change that attitude, or you may be a worthless silver cup. The church's attitude in carrying out its mission and courtship of the Son, cannot be compromised. It is too valuable!

Christ knows that this bride (the church), is the embodiment of who he is and he wants it to be presented to himself in all its glory. Like the man who waits at the altar for his wife to be. That moment, when he hears the processional and his heart begins to pound; when he looks back and sees the woman of his dreams being escorted down the aisle of the church to be given to him as the most perfect gift; it is a glorious sight. What is even better, is when they have saved the best of each other for their honeymoon. They both know that there are no spots, no wrinkles, just a bright future of hope, love and a willingness to face all challenges together. They know that they have done things right. Things that are done the right way end up being on the right path. [*John 14:6 "Jesus saith unto him, I am the way, the truth, and the life: no man cometh unto the Father, but by me."*]

"So ought men to love their wives as their own bodies." Men, if you want a piece of flesh, pay for it at the meat counter in your local supermarket! If you want a wife, then you must be willing to give up a piece of yourself.

When God set out to make a companion for Adam as his wife, he did not look to the animals he had created. He needed substance which would be the same as the man he had created. He did not even think to create a separate being and bring it to him. God in his wisdom, looked at the man as the source to make this companion. God took from him what was necessary to make his help meet. As God looked to the future of the bride for his Son, she had to be a part of who Christ was. So, in the beginning, as He created man, he thought about the church. Man had to give up a piece of himself to have the perfect companion. So too, the church has its perfect companion in Christ Jesus.

Loving your wife as your own body, means taking care of your companion in the same way you take care of your own health. She is not that piece of meat you bought at the supermarket. She is a part of you. She came from you. Stop to think if God had used the DNA of a lion, a mouse, a giraffe, a rhino or orangutan to make your companion. (I'm sure you are going through pictures in your mind just about now.) God made your wife from you, so that you would respect and honor her, because she would be the bearer of your children, the help you needed in carrying out your destiny, in fulfilling your legacy and mandate from God.

"He that loves his wife loves himself." This statement refers back, once again, to the man recognizing that his wife is a part of who he is. Why did you marry your wife in the first place? Did you love her or a part of her? Was it because she was pretty, wise, witty, funny, quirky, good conversationalist, she shared your point of view? Did you just think that she was an easy score and so you appealed to her sentiments? Did you marry her because she was beautiful, smart, had a high standard of values and you respected those values, she respected you and held you to the same set of values?

The Bible is clear. The person that loves his wife, demonstrates that he loves himself. His wife is a reflection of himself. In older couples that have withstood the test of time, you can see that they look more like brother and sister than they do husband and wife. They often don't have to speak as each one understands even the body language. There is mutual respect and admiration. They look more like each other because they love each other.

Instead of looking for negative points to criticize your wife, why not look for positive points to celebrate and acknowledge the wife that you prayed and asked God for? What's that? You did not ask God for your wife? You went out and picked her out yourself? Then, what you see is what you got! When you make your own decisions without consulting God, you are subjected to your own consequences. Self-respect is self-acceptance. It is accepting that your wife and you are one.

"For no man ever yet hated his own flesh; but nourishes and cherishes it, even as the Lord the church." No man wants to die. He takes care of his body by feeding it with good nutrition, exercising, working out, feeding his mind, being spiritually sound, morally straight, trustworthy. To cherish is to love. To love one's self is to hold yourself in high esteem. If this is what you do for yourself, you should do this for your wife as well. The Lord does this for the church; his bride; his wife. He nourishes her and cherishes her. What this is saying is, that if the Lord sets the example, so should His creation follow the same example. If you can't do this, then you don't acknowledge God.

"For we are members of his body, of his flesh, and of his bones." Adam praised God when he received his help meet. He said this was now bone of his bone and flesh of his flesh. It is through Christ that the church is born. It receives the

love and nourishment it requires from him. Therefore, we are members of Christ's body, we are his flesh and we are his bone. We are the expression of Christ in a physical form. He dwells in us. We are intimate with him.

As the church, we are his bride and his body. He is our sustenance and husband. How can we not honor and respect? In riches and in poorness, in sickness and in health, in good times as well as in bad times, for better or for worse. As wife and husband we took a vow, just as Jesus has done for the church.

"Nevertheless, let every one of you in particular so love his wife even as himself; and the wife see that she reverence her husband." The Apostle Paul, summarizes his statements in a twofold admonition in the marriage relationship between husband and wife and the Church Body.

Love your wife as you love yourself. By doing this, then the second part of the statement comes into play. The wife will see fit to reverence her husband.

Below I have introduced one of the best exemplary Biblical treatises on love. Pay close attention to the last three sentences because they underscore the true relationship in love.

BONE OF MY BONES and FLESH OF MY FLESH / 168

25

TRUE LOVE
- 1 JOHN 4

"Beloved, believe not every spirit, but try the spirits whether they are of God: because many false prophets are gone out into the world. Hereby know ye the Spirit of God: Every spirit that confesses that Jesus Christ is come in the flesh is of God: And every spirit that confesses not that Jesus Christ is come in the flesh is not of God: and this is that spirit of antichrist, whereof ye have heard that it should come; and even now already is it in the world.

Ye are of God, little children, and have overcome them: because greater is he that is in you, than he that is in the world. They are of the world: therefore speak they of the world, and the world hears them. We are of God: he that knoweth God hears us; he that is not of God hears not us. Hereby know we the spirit of truth, and the spirit of error.

Beloved, let us love one another: for love is of God; and every one that loves is born of God, and knoweth God. He that loves not knoweth not God; for God is love. In this was manifested the love of God toward us, because that God sent his only begotten Son into the world, that we might live *through him. Herein is love, not that we loved God, but that he loved us, and sent his Son to be the propitiation for our sins. Beloved, if God so loved us, we ought also to love one another. No man hath seen God at any time. If we love one another, God dwells in us, and his love is perfected in us. Hereby know we that we dwell in him, and he in us, because he hath given us of his Spirit.*

And we have seen and do testify that the Father sent the Son to be the Savior of the world. Whosoever shall confess that Jesus is the Son of God, God dwells in him, and he in God. And we have known and believed the love that God hath to us. God is love; and he that dwells in love dwells in God, and God in him.

Herein is our love made perfect, that we may have boldness in the Day of Judgment: because as he is, so are we in this world. There is no fear in love; but perfect love casts out fear: because fear hath torment. He that feareth is not made perfect in love. We love him, because he first loved us. ***If a man say, I love God, and hates his brother, he is a liar: for he that loves not his brother whom he hath seen, how can he love God whom he hath not seen? And this commandment have we from him, that he who loves God love his brother also.*"**

SEXUAL INTIMACY AND CHILDREN

[*Genesis 2:24* "*Therefore shall a man leave his father and his mother, and shall cleave unto his wife: and they shall be one flesh.*"] The intimacy between a man and a woman requires privacy. It requires that the couple be able to express themselves beyond words, into the free expression of the mind, body and spirit. The need to come together in agreement, is not just for the pleasurable enjoyment of both souls but to create an atmosphere of such intense love, that they are willing to bring forth new life. This new life needs to know that it was created in perfect harmony, in the intertwining of souls, in privacy, in the full expression of two loving people who are willing to show the world and give them the best that they can, in terms of a new life. The best of him and the best of her.

There is a difference in reproduction and procreation. All life forms reproduce in one form or another. Humans are meant to procreate. Procreation involves the work of the Holy Spirit. You may think, what do you mean by that? In the natural course of reproduction, there is no soul involved but in the act of procreation there is a soul involved. Men or women who procure sex for their own selfish desires, will often reproduce. In so doing, they don't particularly care if there is an offspring or not. It is an act of self-gratification. For this reason, sometimes end of life for a baby, abortion or just plain murder of innocent lives, is upheld before civil courts; but be fully aware, God keeps inventory of these lives that were born out of selfish desires and then put to death. There will be a day of judgement.

In procreation, the Holy Spirit is present because that is God's way of welcoming new life (Children). He is in favor of new life. He ordered it to happen. He was specific with Adam and Eve. His commandment has not stopped to this day; "be fruitful and multiply". Each new life is a new soul. From the moment the egg is fertilized within the woman, the genetic code for new life kicks in and a soul is created. A consciousness of order and design begins to ensue. There is perfect timing for development of a heart, lungs, body, legs, arms, feet, eyes, nose, hair, ears, cardiovascular, respiratory, nutritional and neurological and a host of other systems that make up the complex being, called a human. This process starts with intimacy at the spiritual level, through the physical biological expression and only stops at the point of physical death.

All life is dear to God. It comes from him and returns to him. As Christ has intimacy with his bride…the church experiences growth in spiritual children. God adds to the church those that will be saved. [*Acts 2:47* "*…And the Lord added to the church daily such as should be saved.*"]

> All life is dear to God. It comes from him and returns to him. As Christ has intimacy with his bride...the church experiences growth in spiritual children. God adds to the church those that will be saved.

Procreation is dear to the Triunity because this is in the Master Plan.

Intimacy is a healthy and integral part of the marriage. It is so critical, that instructions are given in the New Testament.

> [1 Corinthian 7:5 *"Do not deprive one another, unless it is with consent for a time, so that you may give yourselves to fasting and prayer. And come together again so that Satan does not tempt you for your incontinence."*]

Let me interject at this time, that the above verse has a natural as well as a spiritual connotation. The spiritual connotation is visible in the writing. The natural connotation is in the interpretation from the original scripts.

The word fasting means abstinence. It refers to a time, a season away from food, other pleasures or circumstances. It could mean personal, private, alone time, which is necessary for both man and woman. It could be vacation time. It could be a time of illness which requires recuperation. It does not mean however, that it is an excuse for not meeting your conjugal responsibilities with your spouse.

It is a timeframe for affronting diverse situations that require meditation, seeking direction from God. In a sense, you are fasting, you are abstaining. The important factor here is, that you and your spouse have talked it over. You have agreed on a time frame and you have agreed to resume your conjugal responsibilities as soon as possible. The prolongation of this fasting beyond the agreed upon time, will give way for the mind to wander. It will yield to the enemy…Satan if you will…a time and a line of questioning which may lead to rupture in the marriage relationship if for nothing else, truth and trust.

KEEPING IT TOGETHER

The marriage relationship is meant to be permanent. Jesus was questioned on this and here is what he had to say:

[*Matthew 19:3-12* "Some Pharisees came to him to test him. They asked, "Is it lawful for a man to divorce his wife for any and every reason?" "Haven't you read," he replied, "that at the beginning the Creator 'made them male and female,' and said, 'For this reason a man will leave his father and mother and be united to his wife, and the two will become one flesh'? So they are no longer two, but one. Therefore what God has joined together, let man not separate." "Why then," they asked, "did Moses command that a man give his wife a certificate of divorce and send her away?" Jesus replied, "Moses permitted you to divorce your wives because your hearts were hard. But it was not this way from the beginning. I tell you that anyone who divorces his wife, except for marital unfaithfulness, and marries another woman commits adultery." The disciples said to him, "If this is the situation between a husband and wife, it is better not to marry." Jesus

> *replied, "Not everyone can accept this word, but only those to whom it has been given. For some are eunuchs because they were born that way; others were made that way by men; and others have renounced marriage because of the kingdom of heaven. The one who can accept this should accept it."*]
>
> [*Matthew 19: 16-19 "Now a man came up to Jesus and asked, "Teacher, what good thing must I do to get eternal life?" "Why do you ask me about what is good?" Jesus replied. "There is only One who is good. If you want to enter life, obey the commandments." "Which ones?" the man inquired. Jesus replied, 'Do not murder, do not commit adultery, do not steal, do not give false testimony, honor your father and mother,' and 'love your neighbor as yourself."*]

When the question was asked of Jesus in the culture of his time, men were divorcing women for just about any reason. The originators of the question were a religious group called the Pharisees who were real sticklers for the interpretation of the letter of the law. Jesus answered them by quoting Scripture verbatim. When they tried to evade his answer by bringing Moses into the picture, Jesus sets them straight stating that the reason Moses allowed divorce was because their hearts were hard. Jesus presented to them, that the only true reason for divorce is marital unfaithfulness.

I implore the reader to understand that the hardness of the hearts of men, has not changed and perhaps it has become even harder. The laws governing divorce away from the culture that gives us the law and the commandments, have been instituted because of the abuses that have taken place at many levels in society. Although we are not governed by Jewish law, as Christians, we are governed by God's law which comes from a Jewish heritage. The true church, as an organization, still maintains the sanctity of marriage and defends it against divorce as Jesus stated, except for infidelity or adultery.

Even in such a case as infidelity or adultery, if the partners are willing to forgive and go through counseling, every effort should be made to restore the marriage. The church, is called to be an agent of restoration.

My views on the subject, are not to give anyone an excuse for divorce. Each case may have mitigating life threatening circumstances, which could have grievous consequences for a husband, wife or children. In such cases, divorce may be the safest outcome.

Issues such as incest, physical abuse, verbal abuse, death threats to anyone in a marital relationship is certainly not of God. Waiting for God to respond, when we know the correct course of action to take, is as much a sin, as allowing the death of a family member or family members by staying in a marriage relationship that is not what God intended.

On the other hand, simply divorcing because of reasons that could be treated through counseling, therapy or some other professional intervention, will rest on the conscience of the marriage partner.

If you or your wife were the ones making the decisions about your marriage and God was not involved; if you have hit a snag in your relationship that even after counseling, it can't be resolved, then the decision of a divorce is yours and the consequences of that decision are also yours. However, I recommend before finalizing any relationship, that you give God an opportunity. There are men and women of God that can help, through Biblical counseling. The Word of God says: [*Luke 11:9 "Seek and ye shall find, Knock and the door will be opened, Ask and it will be given unto you."*] At this juncture of your life, you have nothing to lose and a lifetime to gain.

If you became a believer somewhere in your marriage relationship and your partner is not, that is insufficient grounds for a divorce.

> [*1 Corinthians 7:12-16 "But to the rest speak I, not the Lord: If any brother hath a wife that believeth not, and she be pleased to dwell with him, let him not put her away. And the woman which hath a husband that believeth not, and if he be pleased to dwell with her, let her not leave him. For the unbelieving husband is sanctified by the wife, and the unbelieving wife is sanctified by the husband: else were your children unclean; but now are they holy. But if the unbelieving depart, let him depart. A brother or a sister is not under bondage in such cases: but God hath called us to peace. For what knoweth thou, O wife, whether thou shalt save thy husband? or how knoweth thou, O man, whether thou shalt save thy wife?"*]

As a believer, you take on the responsibility of the priesthood. You must do what Jesus taught: Love that partner onto salvation. It may take some time for faith to come into your partner's life, maybe because before you met the Lord, you were not trustworthy and that, set you apart. Don't give up. You must show her that Christ is really in you by your love, grace and forgiving attitude. Be willing to be crucified. In saving your partner, you will bare testimony of the power of God, the power of His Word and the generational impact it will have in your home, your community, your church and future generations. God is in the business of miracles on a daily basis. There is nothing impossible for Him.

The church has a responsibility to educate young people and even married couples, on the correct Biblical principles for marriage and the marriage relationship. Hopefully this book will point many young people and couples in the right direction. It will help others to get on the right path in appreciating their partner. Still with others, it may provide an opportunity to seek help, in order to present Jesus his true church bride.

BONE OF MY BONES and FLESH OF MY FLESH / 180

CHURCH LEADERSHIP AND THE MARRIAGE RELATIONSHIP

The Apostle Paul, when writing to his protégé, Timothy, says the following:

[*1 Timothy 3:1-7 "This is a true saying, if a man desire the office of a bishop, he desires a good work. A bishop then must be blameless, the husband of one wife, vigilant, sober, of good behavior, given to hospitality, apt to teach; Not given to wine, no striker, not greedy of filthy lucre; but patient, not a brawler, not covetous; One that rules well his own house, having his children in subjection with all gravity; (For if a man know not how to rule his own house, how shall he take care of the church of God?) Not a novice, lest being lifted up with pride he fall into the condemnation of the devil. Moreover he must have a good report of them which are without; lest he fall into reproach and the snare of the devil."*]

Let's review point by point, this valuable information that not only applies to the church, but first needs to apply to the family that makes up the church.

This is a true saying - The first thing he says is, that there is truth in what he is about to advice. Paul uses the term bishop, because it is the highest form of leadership in the local church structure. He is saying that if you are seeking to work in the church and eventually obtain the highest form of leadership, it is good when you set your spiritual goals that high. However, in performing this good work for God, there is a job description that you need to meet, in order to qualify and eventually be promoted to fill that position.

The interesting thing about Paul's advice is, the order of the qualifications. You will see why once you read on.

A bishop then must be blameless - Paul begins the job description by stating that the bishop must be blameless. Blame is the result of accusations for any number of reasons. So if you are to be held blameless, it would mean, that your past performance, must not provoke the accusations from people, who have known you long enough, to testify about your character and integrity. This covers pretty much your life, from childhood to your present state and the character and nature of the responsibility of the job you are seeking. This does not mean that you are squeaky clean. Clearly the Bible states that we have all sinned and come short of the glory of God. [*Romans 3:23 "For all have sinned, and come short of the glory of God;"*] We are talking about that even if you have wronged someone, performed less than average in your life and the grace of God has reached you; you have become a child of God and he has forgiven you. You must also have forgiven yourself and forgive those that you have wronged. You must have made restitution to the point that, should there be any blame for which you need to take ownership, you can then be accountable and blameless. Keep in mind that in the visibility of the position you wish to discharge, someone you have forgiven, has not forgotten. Being blameless, starts at home with your wife and your children. They can be your fiercest defenders or your most avid accusers. They are your first congregation...your first ministry. The bride must be spotless!

The husband of one wife. You lead by example. Christianity is not a religion. It is a lifestyle. You have to live it, in order to model it.

Being the husband of one wife, is to follow the Biblical model set by God and Christ. It is the fidelity of Christ for his Church. Although there may be many belief systems worldwide, there is only one church which is the bride of Christ.

> You lead by example. Christianity is not a religion. It is a lifestyle. You have to live it, in order to model it.

On a more personal level, we need to understand that the willingness to serve at the highest level of the church leadership, does not allow for promiscuous behavior. There are men in service to God, whose wife may have died for some reason when they were young and have since remarried. This does not disqualify them. They are still married to one woman. If the poor man happens to lose his second wife to any act of God and this is his third wife, does it disqualify him? Certainly not! He is still married to one woman.

The reference by the Apostle is, in being married to one woman and NOT carrying on extra-marital affairs with other women at any level. Marriage is about fidelity. History in the Bible and natural history shows the consequences of multiple relationships outside of marriage and the disastrous consequences with lifetimes of damage and generational curses.

The question begs to be asked: What about a divorced man? A divorced man should be married to one wife and not living with one wife and receiving "fringe benefits" from the other. The reasons for the divorce, have to be looked into with much wisdom and guidance from the Triunity. A pattern of divorce, has to be looked into. The person who aspires to be bishop, is going to be looked at and sought after, for advice on the most prominent ministry of the church: the family. Any pattern, outside of being the husband of one wife, will not be beneficial to the Church of God. The local assembly and leadership, as well as the person aspiring for service in ministry, need to carefully and prayerfully consider their role of leadership in the church. There are other ministries within the work of the church, which are better suited to the character and nature of service in the Body of Christ.

Be vigilant. The leader has to be on the alert for his own weaknesses, for maintaining the integrity of the home, his family, his children, guests he brings to the house, his vocabulary, what he reads, what he watches, where he goes, his role in the public eye, his relationship with other leaders and congregations that he visits. A good wife, is the best armor bearer for the leader. What he can't see because of his male nature, the wife can see, from a female perspective. The enemy is no respecter of how holy you may be, to strike at you with some form of temptation.

Be sober. To be sober is to be of sound mind. To be able to think clearly, in order to execute the responsibility of decisions, made both at home and in service to God. Sober, as in the opposite of being drunk. Just think of any emergency in the home or in the church. If you are not sober, you may not be able to make a prudent decision in order to save a life. The mind needs to be clear and ready to receive instruction from God, to interpret the Word and to deliver with precision its message.

The nature of good behavior, is not just being good. It is about representing the best of social graces at every secular and spiritual event. It speaks to the demeanor of representing the highest standards of the Kingdom; first at home then in the temple.

Given to hospitality. Being hospitable, is how well you treat those that come to your door at home. How well you receive them. How well you represent that you are a servant of the Most High God. How well does your family receive and accept your guests. Your house, may well be the portal for the congregation God may place in your hands. Do you have what it takes to entertain guests? Those that are holy and those that are not. You may be entertaining angels or Jesus himself in another guise.

A word of caution: Your House and God's House need to be respected by anyone that comes through its doors. Not everyone that says Lord, Lord comes in the name of Jesus. Set appropriate rules about hours of visitation. Teach people to respect your time of preparation for service to God. Set time apart from all other business to be with your family. Do not be afraid to politely explain to someone that you have a previous engagement. Be determined to be on time. Time is a God given investment that, once spent, it can't be recovered. Do not be so holy that you neglect taking care of your spouse. Not everything is spiritual or of a spiritual nature. Remember that to everything, there is a season and a time for pleasure under heaven.

Apt to teach. Everyone can communicate a lesson, even if they are a fool. It takes discipline to be a teacher. It is of no value to you, having read the Bible and not put to use its valuable lessons. The first sign of a true believer is, wanting to know more about the Christ that just saved his life for eternity. The evidence for having acquired that knowledge, is behavior modification. That means that your lifestyle should change in accordance with Biblical principles. The Apostle Paul said: "I no longer live but Christ lives in me." The change in your life needs to be communicated. It is called a testimony. Testimonies in court are never based on hearsay. They are based on facts. Teaching, is being able to receive the facts and convey them in such a way, that the listener comprehends what you are saying and obtains the same or if not, better results than yourself. The key to teaching is patience. Teaching is a form of effective communication. The teacher will always be reading. He or she needs to accumulate and understand information in order to process it and pass it on. You can't give what you don't have! At home, your wife and children, expect you as the head of the house, to provide instruction about many things. You need to prepare them for every contingency over which God has permitted you to acquire knowledge. Because their needs change from day to day, you also need to learn from day to day. If you can't manage this at home, how well do you think you can manage this in God's house which is bigger and more complex?

Not given to wine. The communion table is not your local bar. In the navy there is an expression which says that "loose lips sink ships". Wine and Sunday sermons don't mix. Neither does Sunday dinner with a drunken spouse. A glass of wine can be medicinal. Three or more, can be detrimental. Different cultures have different approaches to drinking. Be wise! You represent the nature and character of your own home as well as, and most importantly, the nature and character of God's home. As stated before, remaining sober, allows you to think, analyze and react with prudence and not foolishness. Notice that the Apostle did not say do not drink. He said not given to wine. If in your lifetime you may have been or have had a family member who was or is an alcoholic, you understand the incoherent nature and disrespect of someone under the influence. God heals. The individual and the family need to be sure to have the conscience to prevent alcohol consumption through prevention by avoiding temptation.

Save the family and save the church.

Not a striker. Many a home has been the witness to abusive parents, husbands and wives who are physically abused by their spouses. Children's lives that have been affected by being witnesses to such cruel behavior. The sad part is, that it takes place even in "Christian" homes. Leadership roles in the church need to be considered in lieu of background checks for its members. The Gospel of Jesus is not about boxing a few rounds with your wife or children and then singing songs and praises on Sunday. It is not about terrorizing the family under the threat of corporal punishment. Check your attitude and your boxing diploma into the hands of Jesus. Your family needs love, compassion, understanding and for you to represent Christ as the priest in your home.

Not greedy of filthy lucre. Not the type of person that takes advantage of people's money, makes money illegally or scams people of their wealth. Not the type of person that makes or spends money gambling. Good values are the cornerstone of the family. The priest of the house has to earn an honest living. It is Biblical that by the sweat of your brow, you will earn your keep in order to feed your family. God himself worked six days to create heaven and earth. He went even further by making a garden. There are no shortcuts to an honest living. Anything that is not earned honestly, disappears just as quickly as it came. Do not try and squeeze money from your family and much less from the congregation that God has allowed you to minister.

Patient. Impatience leads to mistakes, impaired

judgment, doing the same things repeatedly, it costs you time and money, ruins friendships and marriages, isolates people and the list can be much longer. Impatience is driven by poor time management and selfish desires; all of which lead to stress. It produces toxins in the body that will at least give you ulcers and eventually kill you.

We hear it all the time, "patience is a virtue". Do we really know what it means? It says that patience is a good moral characteristic, it is a good attribute to your character. The best way I can define patience is having the moral and mental strength to wait. (Some of you reading this, may have other more graphic ways of describing it.)

In the home, patience is so in demand, that you need a supply of it every hour. Patience does not take days or hour or minutes off. Patience is manageable. You need to practice it and it is one of those human attributes that really tests your resolve with God. I think God has a special warehouse just to dispense patience.

Not a brawler. In other words, not looking for arguments or creating them. Not a nagger. The brawler is always reading between the lines. He questions the intent of words because the interpretation being received is negative, derogatory to his character, belief system, or what seems to be right or wrong. The brawler is like a bully about anything you say. The priest of the house, the leader to be in the congregation of the saints is not a brawler. That person allows God to settle the ignorance.

Not covetous. To covet is to wrongfully desire what

belongs to others. Strangely enough coveting has its positive side. Biblically you can covet prayers. In other words, you desire people to pray for you.

On the negative side you cannot covet your neighbor's wife or husband, his or her car, his or her house, etc. Be content with what God has given you. He knows your needs and wants even before you ask for them. Psalm 23 says *"The Lord id my shepherd, I shall not want."* It means that because he is your shepherd and you are his sheep, there is nothing that you need because he will supply your "want".

Rules well his own house. To rule means to govern. It means to promote order. It means to establish rules and regulations for the safety and wellbeing of those that are a part of, who enter or exit your home. When you have a benevolent Ruler, there is harmony in the kingdom. When you have a tyrant or dictator, there is upheaval, chaos, mistrust, pillage, disenchantment and revolts. No one wants to live there. It is the same in the house of God. You can't have leaders that don't govern well. If you want someone that governs well for a leadership role, ask his neighbors to tell you how your candidate manages the property he lives in and how he treats his wife and kids. He may be a saint in church but a tyrant when he gets home.

Having his children in subjection with all gravity. The home is the training ground for the next generation. If as parents we do not do our jobs well, the next generation will take advantage, revenge or mistreat us because we did not do what we were supposed to do. When we say "this new generation doesn't know what they are doing", what we are saying in essence is that we didn't prepare them correctly to take care of us in our senior years. Stop to think what kind of leaders we will have in our churches, when the very premise for respect of the priest of the house, has never been taught or practiced. Your child reflects your power and authority. He/she reflects your government, your prejudices, your biases, your love, your respect for life and your attitude towards the world and it leaders.

>[*Proverbs 22:6 "Train up a child in the way he should go: and when he is old, he will not depart from it."*]

[*Ephesians 6:4 "And, ye fathers, provoke not your children to wrath: but bring them up in the nurture and admonition of the Lord."*] The word provoke as used in the text means "anger". It is, repeated below. Parents - learn how to discipline you child as to correction or modification of the negative behavior exhibited. Yelling, screaming, calling them stupid or making derogatory remarks about their behavior will come back to bite you later on in life. Praise, love, motivate, hug, kiss, celebrate, reward; instigate the positive. This is what your heavenly father does for you. Your earthly father or mother may not have done their job correctly or they did it to the best of their abilities but you have a heavenly father who is ready, willing and able, to get you past the most difficult stages of your life.

>[*Colossians 3:21 "Fathers, provoke not your children to anger, lest they be discouraged."*]

Not a novice. You can't have someone who is a baby

ruling the church of God. In the same way, you can't have the children governing the house. It is hard enough to get a child to run an errand for you. How much more difficult is it, when you have a leader that doesn't even understand Biblical principles and he or she is made a deacon, usher, treasurer, secretary or whatever other vacancy you have in the house of God. We are not running a secular business, we are about the eternal business of the Lord.

Train, educate, prepare, mentor, oversee, discipline and when they are ready, slowly work them into the business of the Kingdom. When you are faithful in the little then you will be promoted to the much. Do not overwhelm your new officers with a lot of responsibility. It goes back to being apt to teach.

Lastly, A good report of them which are without. This goes back to what I said before about a potential leader's testimony within the community he lives in. A person may be very active in the church. He may be wonderful with the congregation. He may be a great armor bearer for the pastor. However, when he gets home, he can't get along with his wife and children. He is abusive, belligerent, argues with his neighbor; he is totally a different person. So he may make a newcomer to the church feel welcome but he will never get his family or neighbors to come to the Lord. He cancels out the good work in the house of God, with the terrible job of the report of them which are without the church community.

In closing out this chapter, allow me to bring your attention to the Apostle Paul's admonition to Timothy.

[*1 Timothy 5:8 "But if any provide not for his own, and especially for those of his own house, he hath denied the faith, and is worse than an infidel."*]

Any person that does not provide for his family, especially those of his own house, he cancels out the faith, the Triunity in his life. He is worse than a sinner.

Your family, your home, should be the first church and the first congregation that you learn to Pastor. It should be a place of peace and one that welcomes the God sent, to receive their first taste of the good news of Jesus Christ. Your home is your first ministry. Review the requirements for being a leader in the church. Look to see if there are areas of your ministry that need repair or restoration. We are not born with all the skills to become the person God needs to work for his Kingdom. But God has provided the resources required and the mentors to help us acquire and polish those skills until we can perform them well and with excellence. Be humble. Ask, seek and knock. Humbleness has the power to bring the proud to their knees; sometimes by conviction and other times by conditions.

BONE OF MY BONES and FLESH OF MY FLESH / 194

29

AN APPEAL FROM CHRIST TO ALL MEN

[1 Peter 3:7 "Likewise, ye husbands, dwell with them according to knowledge, giving honor unto the wife, as unto the weaker vessel, and as being heirs together of the grace of life; that your prayers be not hindered."]

Your Mom.

My brothers, with the exception of Adam, we all come from a woman. The weaker vessel. The one person who carried us to full term of nine months. Through her womb, we were sustained in life, protected, meticulously cared for and all the time, sacrificing what she ate, her housework, taking care of dad, possibly taking care of our other brothers and sisters. She went to the market, did the laundry, prepared food and an endless number of household chores, while we still had no idea of the world outside. We kicked, we fussed, and we made her get up at differing times of the night, just so that we could go to the bathroom. She took precautions by going to the Doctors and checking on our health and hers, just to make sure we were healthy.

When the time came for us to leave the womb, she made sure we had a warm place to sleep, she suckled us, laughed and played with us. She spoke to us, told us about our futures, she sang to us, she took us out wherever she went. She introduced us to people we did not know. She was always present when we cried. She stayed up when we were sick. She made sure we were comfortable and gave us attention when we cried, even for unknown reasons. She loved us regardless of what we looked like, what handicap we came into the world with and we were never without an expression of her love. I want you to reflect on these moments because you seem to have forgotten, the role a woman played in your life.

The Lord reminds you: "you have forsaken my commandment to honor your father and mother. She may be old or feeble. You don't write, you don't call, and you don't remember her birthday or any special moments of her life to honor her. You only remember her when you don't have a place to stay, or you need money or you need food. As an adult you can't stand when she gives you advice. You have heard her so often, that it annoys you. You say you are not a child anymore, but mom is only mom when you need something. You don't seem to remember much about the woman who birthed you, but she can remember all the details of your life as you were growing up and still, has a place for you in her heart.

What kind of a son are you? Don't you think that the woman that was God's instrument for you to come into this world, merits respect? If you have no honor for your mother, how can you honor your wife? You can say all you want about your mother but the fact that you can speak, walk, go to the toilet, can hold a spoon to your mouth, tie your shoe laces, were able to go to school and so much more, is possible thanks to your mother.

Your circumstances at home may have changed, because of your parents. Mom and dad may have had their differences. You ended up an orphan. Perhaps you were abandoned. Only you and God know the circumstances of your life. You still came to the world through a woman.

Your Responsibility to Your Wife

In the Biblical quotation at the beginning of this chapter, the Apostle Peter coaches the believer on the responsibilities of the husband to the wife. We will review his statement carefully because there is something Christ wishes to inform you about your companion, in terms of your home, ministry and the church.

Christianity is the only faith base, which honors the woman in accordance with Biblical principles. Under every other system of religion, woman has been regarded as in every way, inferior to man. Christianity teaches that, in respect to her highest interests, the interests of the Lord God, she is in every way, man's equal. She is entitled to all the hopes and promises imparted by God's Word. She is redeemed in the same way her husband is. She is addressed in the same language of tender invitation. She has the same privileges and comforts which the Word imparts in this world, and in heaven, she will be raised to the same levels.

When the woman is recognized for her value, by making her the equal of man in the hope of heaven, she will rise to her appropriate place. The home will be made to what it should be, a place of intelligence and genuine friendship. A world of suffering and sadness, will smile under the blessing of a Christian woman.

> Christianity teaches that, in respect to her highest interests, the interests of the Lord God, she is in every way, man's equal. She is entitled to all the hopes and promises imparted by God's Word.

Your wife is, in other and higher respects, equal to you. She has, by the will of God, the same access to the grace of life, of all the blessings in this life and the next, and both of you should live peaceably and quietly one with another. Grace is connected with eternal life. Your wife is an heir of the grace of life as well as you. She may be inferior in brute strength but she is your equal in the most important respect; that she is a fellow-traveler with you to a higher world and that in every way, she is entitled to all the blessings which redemption confers, as much as you.

As the man, you have what she needs: courage and strength and as the woman, she has what you want: beauty and delicacy. God has made both of you equal so that there is really, very little superiority on either side.

You may have difficulty as you begin to process the information provided because you are lacking or were lacking in the instruction as outlined in the Bible. If you consider yourself a man of God, if you hold a position of leadership or aspire a position of leadership in God's house, you need to obey Scriptural counsel.

The Word says to *"dwell"* with your wife. The word tabernacle, as used in the Old Testament for the portable house of God, meant dwelling. It was the place where God dwelled with his people. It was the place of abode. We already covered abiding as submission. The use of *"dwell"* by Apostle Peter, has the same meaning. God was the Supreme High Priest and he dwelled with his people. It was a symbol of the Church and its children, where the husband and wife, dwelled together. As God dwelled with his people and as Christ dwells with the church as its head, so must the man dwell with his wife in his house. Your house is your first church. You are its first priest and your wife is the priestess and first member. See to it that you dwell in harmony.

"According to knowledge". This is the second request in the verse. Dwelling with the wife according to knowledge, is with an intelligent view of the nature of the relation, according to the gospel. It is not according to lust, as some pervert; nor according to passion, as if she were some sex object; but according to knowledge, as a wise and reasonable man, who knows his acceptable responsibility as stated in the Word of God. You ought to behave towards your wife as a man who has the knowledge of God; one who understands the purposes for which marriage was appointed, and the way in which believers should behave in that holy estate. The attention to these details, should

keep you in check from becoming, unkind, unfaithful, or hurtful to her earthly comfort or spiritual development. What kind of gospel are you preaching, in and out of your house?

"Giving honor unto the wife." We have covered this topic throughout the book but it is well worth reiterating. It means giving her the respect she merits; not just as a wife but as a woman of God. It means upholding her authority within the realm of her responsibilities and God given gifts. It means protecting her person; her honor as your wife; supporting her value, taking an interest in her conversation; providing for her personal financial needs, if she is not employed. Giving her the liberty of trust and confidence in herself. No need to set up a GPS or tracking device because you don't trust her.

"As unto the weaker vessel." The woman is called a vessel for various reasons. It may be because the husband uses her as his friend and helper in the active ministries of home and church. It could be because like an earthen vessel she can be easily broken. It could be because of the dwelling place of her soul. It could be because the body is the instrument by which the soul accomplishes its purposes. It could be because as a vessel, she is an instrument; a helper; one who is employed by another to accomplish anything, or to assist him. Perhaps it is because her body is prone to many illnesses to which as a man, you may never be exposed. She may have a great mind equal to your own; she may have moral qualities in every way superior to yours; but the God of nature has made her with a more delicate constitution, a more fragile body.

"That your prayers be not hindered". As the priest of the house, you do not need to ask whether you must establish family worship; you do it as one of the fruits of your relationship with Christ. You don't need a formal command.

The Bible verse does not seem to indicate that prayer has to be together at all times but it does seem to imply the "your" in the statement could mean both husband and wife. It also implies by "prayers", that it could be the prayers of both husband and wife. It may even imply that you may lose your desire for prayer or they, will not have much success.

Why will my prayers be blocked? Because you as the man, fail at not being able to follow the Biblical instructions of responding with respect and honor to your wife. It means that your prayers could be blocked. As it states in the gospel of Matthew: [*Matthew 5: 23, 24 "Therefore if thou bring thy gift to the altar, and there remembereth that thy brother hath anything against thee; Leave there thy gift before the altar, and go thy way; first be reconciled to thy brother, and then come and offer thy gift."*]

BONE OF MY BONES and FLESH OF MY FLESH / 202

30

AN APPEAL FROM CHRIST TO ALL WOMEN

[*Psalm 133:1 "Behold, how good and how pleasant it is for brethren to dwell together in unity!"*]

[*1 Peter 3:1-6 "Likewise, ye wives, be in subjection to your own husbands; that, if any obey not the word, they also may without the word be won by the conversation of the wives; While they behold your chaste conversation coupled with fear. Who's adorning let it not be that outward adorning of plaiting the hair, and of wearing of gold, or of putting on of apparel; but let it be the hidden man of the heart, in that which is not corruptible, even the ornament of a meek and quiet spirit, which is in the sight of God of great price. For after this manner in the old time the holy women also, who trusted in God, adorned themselves, being in subjection unto their own husbands: Even as Sara obeyed Abraham, calling him lord: whose daughters ye are, as long as ye do well, and are not afraid with any amazement."*]

The Triunity says: "dear sisters, please pay attention to the words of my Apostle Peter. I inspired him through my Holy Spirit, to share the following with you all."

"Ye wives, be in subjection to your own husbands that, if any obey not the word, they also may without the word be won by the conversation of the wives." The Biblical order as far as authority, cannot be challenged. It was given by God, written by men and endorsed by Christ. God has the authority over man because man was created by God. The woman was created by God but came from the man. She is then under the authority of man. Christ is the Son of God and so he is under the authority of God. The church is the bride of Christ and so she is under the authority of Christ. By example and commandment, everyone is subject to authority.

When Peter wrote his book, he provided instruction about the relationship between man and woman. When he speaks of wives being in subjection to their husbands, he is saying that because of the order in authority, there should be an affectionate submission to the will, and obedience to the delegated authority, of their own husbands. This obliging conduct, would be the most likely way to model the character and nature of Christ and win those disobedient and unbelieving husbands, who had rejected the Word, or who paid attention to no other evidence of the truth, unless they saw it in the sensible, peaceable, and noteworthy conversation of their wives.

Peter also offers this advice to non-believing women, who had become believers and he did not want them to neglect their duties to their husbands because of the gospel. They were still under authority and now more than before, they needed to willfully submit in order to win their husbands to Christ.

A humble subjection, and a loving, reverent respect, are duties which Christian women owe their good or bad husbands. Though much more difficult now, than they were before, these duties were due from Eve to Adam before the fall, and are still necessary.

> *"Who's adorning let it not be that outward adorning of plaiting the hair, and of wearing of gold, or of putting on of apparel; but let it be the hidden man of the heart, in that which is not corruptible, even the ornament of a meek and quiet spirit, which is in the sight of God of great price."*

Peter continues his orientation for these women who have converted to Christianity by making positive recommendations on behalf of their husbands. His recommendations are also being offered in lieu of prostitutes, who would dress provocatively to lure men. There was nothing wrong with arranging their hair, wearing gold or wearing elegant apparel. However, there was a marked distinction when he says that the adorning should be in the hidden man of the heart.

> A humble subjection, and a loving, reverent respect, are duties which Christian women owe their good or bad husbands.

Christian people should take care, that all their external behavior represents their new lifestyle in Christ. They must be mindful in all manner of conversation. As women who are now under the authority of Christ and their husbands, the outward adorning of the body should not be sensual and excessive; it should be moderate, not drawing attention as to allure or tempt others. It should not be too expensive, revealing or extravagant. You don't want to imitate the levity and vanity of the world. Dress according to good taste which pleases your husband or is required for your status in life.

Your fashion statement should not be something corruptible. It should enhance the work of the Holy Spirit. The external ornaments of the body are destroyed by the moth or oxidation. Most often they fall apart with use but the grace of God, the longer we wear it, the brighter and better it is.

The part to be adorned should be the hidden man of the heart; that is, the soul; the hidden, the inner wo/man. Take care to adorn and beautify your souls rather than your bodies. There is an outward manifested beauty, when the soul rejoices in its Savior. It is most often manifested with a smile, a caring heart, a soft word, a willingness to serve, a meek and gentle spirit and a firm and confident stance that greater is He that is in you than he who is in the world.

> *"For after this manner in the old time the holy women also, who trusted in God, adorned themselves, being in subjection unto their own husbands: Even as Sara obeyed Abraham, calling him lord: whose daughters ye are, as long as ye do well, and are not afraid with any amazement."*

In his concluding statement, Peter speaks of the old time holy women. He is not talking about out of style old hags. He is reverently referring to women in the Old Testament as far back as Sara. They adorned themselves to please their husbands. They willingly submitted to their husbands. Sara is an example: she called her husband lord. Why Sara? Because it was Sarah, whose name was changed by God, from Sarai to Sara. Her name means princess of multitudes. The fact that she was recognized by God as princess, in her own rank, she still obeyed her husband. She followed him when he went from Ur of the Chaldeans, not knowing where he was going, and called him lord. She showed him reverence and acknowledged his superiority over her.

You can try and use the excuse of the weaker sex when it's convenient, but these holy women from old, received recognition because of their submission, even at the time when they lived. Consider: they lived in old time, had less access to information to stay current and fewer examples to encourage them; yet in all ages they performed their obligation; they were "holy women". It is because of what they stood for, that their example needs to be followed; they trusted in God, and yet did not neglect their duty to their husbands. The duties required from you, of a quiet spirit and of subjection to your own husbands, are not new. These are qualities/obligations, which have for ever been practiced by the greatest and best women in the world.

You may have been daddy's little girl or mommy's little princess, but your heritage goes back further than your great, great, great grandma. Your heritage goes back to Eve. If you want to claim your right status in the Kingdom, you must learn from the best. That is why Peter says *"whose daughters ye are, as long as ye do well, and are not afraid with any amazement."* It should not surprise you that you have such an extended heritage. You come from a long line of women of faith and good works. You are courageous and not quitters; you know truth in the Word. You will neither quit the truth you profess, or neglect your obligations to your husband. You will do what you must, without either fear or force. You will do it primarily, out of conscience towards God and sense of fulfillment to God's glory.

GOD'S FAMILY

A Christian lifestyle makes for a happy home. Allow the principles of God's knowledge and wisdom to reign in your family. It will permit Christ, to be the unseen guest in your home. The family that is obedient to the Word of God, that listens to the still voice of the Holy Spirit, appreciates the selfless sacrifice of Christ Jesus, will be the model home for the gospel. It will be one of intelligence, contentment, and peace.

Permitting the Triunity to work through every member of the family, is a simple and easy way of being happy in the family relation. Though there be poverty, and disappointment, and sickness, and cares, and losses, yet there will be peace within, for there will be mutual love, and the cheerful hope of a brighter world. A house is just wood, brick, mortar, concrete, cables and pipes. A home is where the heart hangs its coat and pumps love without reservation to every artery of the life within. No matter how much money you spend on paint for the outside, how expensive your furniture may be, how many servants attend to you, how many festive parties you undertake or the number of cars in your garage, nothing will secure the happiness in your home as with Jesus in your home. When the time comes that you have to face disease, disappointments, death, or whatever the storms of life throws at you, the most valuable asset, is your relationship with your family.

> The family that is obedient to the Word of God, that listens to the still voice of the Holy Spirit, appreciates the selfless sacrifice of Christ Jesus, will be the model home for the gospel.

God takes exact notice, and keeps an exact record, of the actions of all family members in the world. He takes into account the submission of wives to their husbands as an obligation which has been practiced universally, by holy women in all ages. God takes notice of the good that is in his servants, to their honor and benefit, but covers a multitude of failures.

The greatest honor of any man or woman, lays in a humble and faithful behavior of themselves in the relation or condition which may come their way. As Christian families, we should dwell with one another, not out of fear, nor from force, but from a willing mind, and in obedience to the Word of God.

In conclusion, I say this to men and especially Christian men. You are the symbol of Christ in the home and everywhere you go. This should be enough, to be on your guard at all times. For if you hold a position of leadership within the house of God, from Janitor to Bishop, you have a multitude of witnesses watching your every move.

You have a wife and children who not only look up to you, but expect you to treat them as Jesus would. How you treat your wife and children, speaks of the virtues of a wise man in this generation and for the next. You lay the ground work for other believers, the wives of those you mentor, the sons and daughters that will honor and respect you, their wives and husbands by your example.

The community you live in, sees your house as that of a Godly man. How you manage that property and everything that goes on, in and out, represents your good stewardship of what God has given you.

We are not perfect! That stage in our life comes when we come face to face with Christ. But until that moment, before the throne of God, we must elevate our help meet to the standard allowed of all believers by the grace of God unto salvation. You cannot do this work alone. The burden is heavy but the yoke is light. Make your burden lighter. Recognize your wife as a ministry partner. When the gospel you preach, because you live it, reaches her, you will have a willing and active companion. She will be your armor bearer because you not only speak truth but you experience it with her.

My dear collaborators in the work of the Lord. If after reading this, you feel you have fallen short of the mark.

You feel that you have failed your family or your congregation, have the courage to ask for forgiveness. Give the Holy Spirit, an opportunity to elevate you to higher ground. Then, go forward and practice what you preach.

To all women around the world who have read this book, Christ is the only man, Son of God, who has elevated women to his side; not only through salvation but making them a symbol of his church. You have that distinct privilege of his recognition and honor. As a man and servant of God, I apologize to you for the injustices and atrocities that have been committed against you, for the lack in man's understanding of God's Master Plan. Sin nature has affected all of us and the originator of sin has been sentenced by God. Because the first Adam failed, God sent us his only Son, Christ Jesus, the husband of the church and the one who understands very well, the role of women and wives in his Kingdom.

Moving forward with Christ in your hearts, know that all men will eventually be judged by Christ. Your self-sacrifice in submission to the Biblical principles of marriage will help to change the tide of brute, masochistic and evil men who will burn in hell for their rebellious nature of not surrendering their hearts to the Lord of lords and King of kings. Like Queen Esther, you will be exonerated. You will be given a crown of life. Every tear will be avenged. Every wound will be healed. Every scar will be tenderly erased. Every child you ever lost, will see you in heaven. The glories of your victories will forever be told in the presence of God. Even though you are considered the weaker vessel, you are the prettiest, the most used; you hold the best fragrances and the best wines. Your vessel will never remain empty in the presence of God. Good men will also come to recognize this. Rejoice, rejoice for your Redeemer lives and the glory of his light shall reach you no matter in what dark corner of this planet man wants to hurt or hide you.

Humanity's understanding of relationship, has prepared the way for Jesus and the church. The church is a part of Jesus. He gave birth to it. That is why all relationship of God's children to the church, has its foundation in family. Everything that man has done to break up the family, takes away from our relationship to God the Father, Jesus and the church. This is why we have been called to restore the family. In doing so, we restore the church. We heal the bride of the Lamb and we can present her without blemish to the second Adam which is Christ.

> [*Matthew 11:28 "Come unto me, all ye that labor and are heavy laden, and I will give you rest."*]

The End

www.ingramcontent.com/pod-product-compliance
Lightning Source LLC
LaVergne TN
LVHW051552070426
835507LV00021B/2546